Choose Me

"Perceiving and Believing in Your Own Value and Purpose"

By: Angelic Chloe

Table of Contents

Chapter Four: Honor the Process/Honor the Way

Chapter Five: Commit to Choosing "You", While Choosing Christ First

Dedication:

First and foremost, I dedicate this book and my life to Yaweh, JESUS CHRIST, my Lord and Savior-my best friend, my first love and the Lover of my soul. God is my everything and He is more than worthy of my praise. He has been so good to me and still is. There would be no Angelic Chloe, without Jehovah, Jesus, or Holy Spirit! So, to God of my world, my heart, my soul, my everything-Thank you! This book has been and is a true form of worship to my King. May He and His name forever be exalted and glorified!

Secondly, I dedicate this book to my Mother, Elizabeth and to my Aunt Stella, who has been like a second mother to me all my life. These two women of God, next to God, have immensely shaped me into the person that I am today. I thank God for blessing me with you both. Your words, your presence and your essence have always been a mainstay in my life. You both are strong and resilient, God-fearing women. I praise God for you two, not only in the book, but in life; I honor you-Mother Elizabeth. I honor you Mother Stella. I pray the bountiful blessings of God in and upon you. May God graciously restore and multiply unto you all that you have poured out over the years. For surely, your work, nor your life has never been in vain. You both are great and because of you two, I now walk in my own greatness! Thank you for everything and more!

I also dedicate this book to my brother Rasheed, who recently went home to glory with The Lord. Rasheed, you have always been such a great person, and your life has forever changed how I see life. God has shown me, through your walk and life with Him, the true definition of purpose and greatness. You, great man of God, will forever live in my heart. Thank you for helping me to get to where I am today. I will always love you. I honor you, Man of God. Fly high and rest in eternity in the bosom of our Lord.

I also dedicate this book to my sister and my other brother, Rose and Hayden. Thank you for your support and love. I honor you both in this book and in life. To all three of my siblings, here is to the birth of a greater legacy! May Rasheed's legacy live on through us and every life that he has impacted. May God show you both favor and prosperity, riches and wealth. I pray many blessings upon you, and may you both walk out God's greatness in your life-living up to God's full potential in you.

I dedicate this book to my friend, and sister, Stephanie. I thank God for you and your beautiful, selfless heart. I pray that God bestows upon you great riches and prosperity, as well as, everything that your heart desires. Thank you for always being there for support and encouragement. Continue to pursue the greatness that God has placed within you! I will not say that you will be great one day, because in the eyes of God, you are already Great! Walk into and own it girl!

Lastly, I dedicate this book to all of my family, friends and relatives, who have played a part in my story. I pray that my journey and greatness will be a catalyst of inspiration for you to walk in your own greatness that God has equipped in you. Know that, not even the sky is the limit. You all will do great things!

I dedicate this book to all of the future blessings waiting for me and for my future legacy!

I dedicate this book to all of the women who will encounter the words on the pages of this book. Here is to your own legacy of greatness!

I love you all! Thank you for your love, encouragement and support!

~ Love Angelic Chloe

Foreword:

We, as Christian women (and women in general) are facing a crucial epidemic: there is a mass majority of women are not manifesting the greatest and full potential that God has created them to manifest; these women are either going to their graves, or are in danger of going to their grave, with such unkept and unfulfilled potential. Their greatness is left unexpressed and un-manifested.

There are 2 key underlying factors which contribute to this travesty:

1. Women do not know who and Who's they are. They do not know their true identity or value.
2. They abort the process necessary to manifest potential and greatness as God has purposed and intended.

In this book, "I Choose Me: Perceiving and Believing in Your Own Value and Purpose", I deal with 2 main topics: Value and Purpose.

Value is then broken down into 2 sub-categories of which I am defining and calling:

A. **Inherent Value**
B. **Added Value**

Inherent value is the value that God has inherently placed within all of us. This value mirrors the reality that God created you and I to be a Queen.

WE are a Royal Diadem, a Royal Priesthood. Whether you are Queen conscious or not, the fact still remains that you are still a Queen. The inherent value that God gives to us all says that we are enough. We are beautiful-fearfully and wonderfully made. We are competent and adequate. We are all things good and the sweet aroma to God's nose. The inherent value speaks to affirmation of our self-esteem, as valued and perceived in the eyes of God.

In this book, you and I will explore how God sees you; this book is a tool to help you get into strategic alignment with God's truthful perception of you, as it relates to your value. We will explore how that central core value and perceived value thereof, then trickles into all areas of your life, including relationships and work. You will read on these pages of real life examples and experiences from my own life of when I did not have a true, authentic concept or perception of my own inherent value, and how that manifested and resulted in some areas of my life. You will learn from parts of my story, and will be encouraged and equipped to transform your own self-perception of your inherent value; You will be challenged to assess areas of your own life.

Added Value is the value that one procures or acquires via the process of pursuing purpose, in route to manifesting greatness and destiny. On top of the inherent value that God naturally places within us, throughout life, we acquire more value during the process toward purpose and greatness. Every stage of purpose has a process that is necessary for equipping us for the next dimension. With every process, once successfully undergone, we obtain what is symbolic to us as jewels added to our crown.

In this book, I will walk you through understanding the process for purpose and help you understand how the process adds value to your already existing inherent value. You will be challenged to grow, but you will also be encouraged, edified and equipped.

"I Choose Me: Perceiving and Believing in Your Own Value and Purpose" is all about correctly perceiving your own value through the right lens, (the eyes of God) and then investing in both your inherent value and your added value. It is about investing in your own worth and your own process in your progress toward manifesting purpose and greatness. Don't wait for others to give you permission to invest in what God has already vested within you. Choose to see and believe in the value that you carry. Be blessed woman of God.

"You are Royal. There is greatness within you and God loves you!"

~ Angelic Chloe

Prelude:

Often times in life, we sit around in passivity, as we wait for others to pick us-whether that be a job, career, relationship, etc. We play that same game that we have played since childhood. You know the one: that game where we stand in a "faceless mass" of people as we wait eagerly to be chosen to join "the team".

The only difference between now and then, is that instead of waiting to be chosen for a baseball team or cheerleading, or kickball, now we are waiting to be chosen as the next team member of our dream job, or the spouse of our dream guy, …etc.

We're waiting to be chosen for a promotion or waiting on someone else to invest in us!

Often times, as we wait, we grow bitter, as we are never chosen. We compare ourselves to the next person, as it becomes everyone else's turn to be chosen. We then question ourselves, "Why not me?" We say to ourselves, "I'm (this quality) or I'm (that quality)." We know that we have what it takes! Why can't others see our value and "take a chance" on us? We think to ourselves, "if only they would just take a chance on me, they would see that I am worthwhile."

We even get creative in ways that we would increase our chances of getting "chosen".

All too often, these creative ways of us "getting noticed" compromises the very value within us.

In an attempt to get others to see our value, we somehow lose perspective and sight of our own value.

This book is to challenge you to see your own value and prompts and encourages you to be your own investor, because you ARE valuable and you are worth investing in!

So, don't wait around for that spouse, that job, that opportunity…etc- You choose "You"-yourself!

Chapter One:
Your New Beginning!

Section One: Embrace Change/Permission Granted!

Chapter One*Embrace Change*Permission Granted*

This chapter is devoted to helping you to let go of the chains that hold you in a perpetual cycle of "what was". You have to let go of past behaviors, experiences, and attitudes, before you can walk into the "newness" of what God has for you.

Too often, we get stuck in a certain way of thinking or a certain way of doing things because that is how we "have always done it", or have always thought that way. Even worse, others around you in your natural circle have forever witnessed these old ways of doing and old way of thinking things; you may feel like you have to live up to that certain "standard" that has already been "established". Therefore, you become afraid and walk in the wrongful fear of embracing change.

You feel like you have to stay the same forever. You feel like you need permission from others to say that it is ok for you to change-for you to walk into the newness that you know that God is calling you into!

Some people will always want you to stay the same, especially if it benefits them in some way. No matter who approves or disapproves the changes you desire to make for the good, you do NOT need their permission. God, who is ultimate Sovereignty and our loving Father and Creator, freely gives you permission to leave behind those old chains and to STEP into the *newness of life*. "Behold, old things are passed away. All things are new".

(2 Corinthians 5:17)

God is challenging you to forever take out the dry and dead skeletons and to step into the fullness of new things. He is calling you into a *Rebirth!*

At a certain point, those skeletons were all you knew; Those skeletons that once had life, and that worked in previous seasons, is now no longer viable in this season of your life. You have outgrown some things! God has even changed some things on the inside of you on a symbolically "skeletal" level. He has rearranged some things, but you are afraid to let your inner circle and the world around you know your new self. You may even struggle internally with how to accept, let alone, embrace the new you- all the Great new things that God has done and is doing in you!

Do not be entangled in fear, beloved. God tells us in 2 Timothy 1:7, "you have not been given the spirit of fear, but of **power, love,** and a **sound mind".** Scripture reminds us in Romans 8:32, "*He that spared not his own Son, but delivered him up for us all, how shall he not with Him, also freely give us all things?*"

Jesus was the ultimate sacrifice and gift to you and us all. He was and *is* God's most **valuable** possession and loved one; and God gave Him freely to you and me. Could you imagine giving your only child? That says a lot about the magnitude of God's love for you and me! It also illustrates this: since Jesus is the ultimate sacrifice, God will freely give us anything else because nothing else even comes close to the value or sacrifice of Jesus!

So, if you are seeking *peace, boldness, comfort, …*etc. God will give it to you. God will comfort you as others reject the new you that they do not understand nor want to understand or embrace.

God will give you boldness to step out and walk into the newness of the life that He created and ordained for you to live since before the foundation of the Earth or the existence of mankind. Do not allow others to ROB you of your birth right of manifesting into the Royal Priesthood that God created you to be!

You do not need their permission nor approval!

Embrace Change! Your permission has been granted!

Galatians 1:10: "Am I now trying to please men, or am I trying to persuade God? If I were trying to please men, then I would not be a servant of Christ."

"Don't let others wrongfully define you. The Author of the world has already written out the definition of your content. God's word is evidence of who you are. There is greatness in you and God loves you!"

~Angelic Chloe

Chapter One: Section Two: Launch Pad

Chapter One * Launch Pad*

In a world where everyone wants to fit in and/or be accepted, we sometimes get caught up in other's opinions of us. We give into the notion that if others are paying attention to us, then we are accepted, thus "validating" our significance.

What is that one thing that you absolutely love to do and have a born passion for? Is it writing? speaking? Artistic works? Teaching? Etc…

Does it validate you or provide you with a sense of importance if others acknowledge your art or craft? You throw yourself, all of your entire being into your craft, hoping to be acknowledged. What if no one-absolutely no one-paid attention? What if no one came to your meticulously orchestrated art exhibit? What if no one read your blog that you poured your heart out into and literally spent hours on-no one cared.

Would you stop doing what you are passionate about because it did not receive the accolades that you had hoped for? I sure hope not. Why? …because you my sister, have a unique set of gifting that God, himself has equipped you with. He has brought you to the Kingdom for such a time as this.

God thought you were so significant that He decided that the world needed one of you-so *He loved you into existence!*

He created you with certain capabilities, passion, and purpose. No one may not seem to care, or maybe they don't, but God cares. If no one else choses you or your work, or whatever you do...CHOOSE YOURSELF!

God has already chosen you, so you're significant by default-you do not need the world's approval or validation! If you are truly passionate about what is within you-whatever that thing is, that you do or speak, (that God has placed within you) then let that truth reign within and through you my sister.

Why should another person's opinion of you be more significant than your own insightful opinion? After all, you know the real you and even more so, God knows you and acknowledges you! He has given you supreme recognition when He calls you by name! "But now, O Jacob, listen to the Lord, who created you. O Israel, the one who formed you says, 'Do not be afraid, for I have ransomed you. I have called you by name; you are mine" (Isaiah 41:3)

So, if no one else favors you or your God given passion, then know that your passion is still real-it is tangible and significant! Choose to be true to your rightful identity. If you are a writer, then write! You don't become a writer just because others suddenly acknowledge you as one. You are first a writer. If you are a speaker, declare yourself as a speaker, and so on, according to that which God, Himself has declared and has placed within you. It all starts with your own self-perception and confidence in your own ability and identity. Hone your craft, work hard and always improve. Your skill level and gifting will eventually meet the title when you are persistent through the process of becoming one with who you are in Christ and what you are meant to do. The Bible tells us in Proverbs 27:3, "so as a man thinks in his heart, so is he." What do you think of yourself?

Whether in life, work, relationships, profession, etc…choose yourself, and others will follow. If they don't, then they are the ones who lose value added to them. *You are valuable and you have value to add!*- This is why God created you- to glorify Him, as you add value to others and self. Don't wait to be chosen-YOU choose "you"-yourself!

Chapter Two:

The Beauty of Value

Chapter Two Intro:

Chapter 2: The Beauty of value is dedicated to challenging you to perceive your real value in CHRIST, and not to settle for anything less in life. This includes relationships, job, career, friendships, and any other area of your life. Know your value in every area of life.

This chapter may appear to skip around to different things, as it addresses romantic relationships, then shifts gears to careers. It is not solely focused on one area, but rather focuses on having true value in all areas of your life. I share with you some of my own personal experiences in different areas and also encourage you in the different areas of your life. Enjoy the read my friend.

~Angelic Chloe

Chapter 2: The Beauty of Value

Know Your Value

When I was younger, I used to *intentionally* put myself "on display", in order to attract a guy-in hopes that he would choose me. I really had no concept or awareness of my own value, and I sought external validation from a man. To me, this was the ultimate form of acceptance and conveyed the idea that if a man chose me, then I was valued and significant. Likewise, if I was not chosen, that sent the message that I was not "valuable enough", nor significant enough.

As I sought, for years through my youth, to be "completed by a man", I found no true fulfillment-as the number of "eligible bachelors" did not come line up at my door. I began to further question my value. Why weren't these guys interested?

I knew that I had something worthwhile to offer, but yet was not mindful of the true value that I possessed. I was willing to give that value away to the first bidder who would affirm that I had value.

Through a sequence of events, I grew closer in intimacy with JESUS CHRIST. He began to unravel me, and for the first time in my life, I saw true value within. I then saw myself through the eyes of GOD and I was *beautiful! I was valued and valuable!* Revelation set in and it then occurred to me that if GOD says that I am worthy and valuable (as He gave His only begotten Son, Jesus, for me and you) then who is man or any other person to declare that I am not worthy? GOD gave the ultimate sacrifice for me and you when He pursued us relentlessly and was obedient even unto death. Philippians 2:8 says, "And being found in fashion as a man, He humbled Himself, and became obedient unto death, even the death of the cross." (KJV)

He gave His life so that you and I could have life, and in that life is found value. If it weren't so, would GOD have gone so far for us? So that was it, value set in. I *knew* my value. I stopped comparing myself to the other girls who had guys.

I will always remember this one particular analogy that further reinforced my concept of value. This is the analogy: it started with the question, "why don't guys choose me?" It beaconed with the answer of a simple apple tree. I am like the bright, shiny and full apple at the top of the tree. Only the harvester who is willing to put in time and effort to climb to the top will ever get the apple, while the lazy and ill-intentioned harvesters pick the apples at the bottom-as they are the most available and convenient. In essence, what the analogy was saying is that I have more value (and so do you) and therefore, in order for a man to deserve me, he must put in the time and effort (and a ring ☺) to secure me.

It turned out that I was like that shiny bright apple that can be seen at the top. It was never that guys did not notice me, but rather the opposite. They noticed the value and standard that I had within myself, and were not willing to commit for the value. They had other ill-intentions and I clearly would not go for that, so they did not even try. Due to the fact that they did not try, it was easy to previously think that it was a case of "not enough value", but on the contrary. So, I will tell you the same thing my sister-you are that shiny, bright and beautiful apple at the top of the tree that requires a man to climb and put in work in order to even reach you.

Don't be so easy and available. I am NOT advocating "playing games". I am simply saying, Know your value and stand proudly in position as the Royal Priesthood (QUEEN) that you are. 1 Peter 2:9 says, "But ye are a chosen generation, a royal priesthood, a holy nation, a peculiar people; that ye should show forth the praises of Him who has called you out of darkness into His marvelous light:".

If you know your value in CHRIST, you won't be so apt and eager to give yourself away to just anyone, except the spouse that GOD gives you. Let me encourage you with this: if you have already given yourself to the wrong person who has not earned your value through the price of marriage, know that GOD still loves you and it is never too late to make a change. Start the right way today. Keep yourself for the right one that GOD has already ordained for you. Sister, don't wait for a man to choose you. Live a full life as a happy and content single. Choose yourself, and first choose the One, who first chose you-JESUS CHRIST.

PRACTICE YOUR VALUE

After some time of me realizing my value in CHRIST, still being human, I yet again started questioning, "where is my husband", as so many of us do, right? This time, I knew I had value and standards, and refused to drop those for any man. I was firm and resolute. Yet, I still wanted to be "found" by "the one". My path crossed with many guys who I refused to settle with.

However, I went through a brief season where I subconsciously put myself on "display". When I met an attractive guy that I actually "liked"-so as to say, "look at me", "here's why you should choose me"....etc.

I would try to broadcast certain characteristics in myself that were there, of which I thought a husband would want or need in a wife. I was much like that old school salesperson who went door to door, trying to convince potential buyers of the value of the product that I carry. I always came on way too strongly-reeking of desperation, trying to "close the deal". I didn't even realize that I was doing this. Does this sound like you?

"Angelic, I thought you said you knew your value?" you might ask. Yes, yes I did *know* my value. I was aware, but I later realized that I did not practice my value. I did not practice that of which I was already aware. You see, while I was no longer desperate to be "hitched" and now had a better sense of my value and had developed standards, (I knew my self-worth in CHRIST for the first time), but there was still a point where I became so excited to share my newly found value. I was now convinced that I had value, but then tried to convince guys of that value. "Is that really knowing your value if you had to convince someone" you may ask. Yes; my value did not diminish. It was simply my presentation of value and how it was perceived that was the key variable here. I knew I had value, but missed the part about how to *present* it.

Let me illustrate: if I gave you a diamond necklace wrapped in a garbage bag, and then filled it with debris and old food, would you want it? Most likely not! However, if I gave you that same diamond necklace, wrapped neatly and nicely in a blue Tiffany's box, maybe even with an inscription, you would definitely or most likely jump to receive it!

It was the same thing with me in the past. I am not comparing myself to garbage, just making an illustration: same content on the inside-different delivery. My value within had not changed; it was simply delivered (presented) incorrectly, which then impacted how guys perceived the package altogether.

Once again, I went deeper with CHRIST, and settled into my true value and received more insight and revelation through HOLY SPIRIT and GOD's love. I went from simply knowing my value, to *practicing* my value. I realized that I am NOT that salesperson who needs to go door to door, begging for the attention of potential "buyers".

I *am* that exquisite artwork that sits at the center of the room and who's beauty and value attracts the "buyer". Let me put this into context with this illustration: Let's say I were a Mercedes Benz, Ferrari or Lexus, or some other high-end luxury vehicle; If a salesperson went door to door trying to convince a potential buyer of the value of that Mercedes or car, the *perceived value* would be much lower than its actual value, than if that same customer went into the dealership and saw that high end vehicle confidently on display in the showroom. This analogy came to me and through it, I realized that when you _know_ your true value and <u>practice</u> your true value, you don't have to present, or put on display, the value speaks for itself, and in turn, attracts the right buyer.

You could have that same Mercedes on Display in the showroom and a Mercedes being sold door to door- which one would you think will sell more? The Mercedes being sold door to door reeks of desperation and its <u>perceived</u> value is therefore diminished. Meanwhile, its <u>actual</u> value stays the same.

I, and you my sister, are like that Mercedes that sits on the platform in all of its glory, where "potential buyers" come to it and not the other way around. Why? Simply because when you *know* and *practice* your value, others know it too!

When you lack a sense of true value, you feel like you have to put yourself on display, door to door, until you find a "buyer". However, when you both *know* your value (have an awareness of) and *practice* (present the right way) you are no longer focused on trying to get attention. You then become focused on being, what I like to call a "lady in living". This is when your perceived value *matches* your actual value and you become focused on living your life with purpose, instead of being obsessed with galivanting in front of men to "be found". What should you be doing?-waiting for someone to notice your value and put a ring on it?...or should you live the life CHRIST died for and intended for you ? (whether someone notices you or not). The latter is on point for sure!

So, let me tell you my sister, I stopped trying to get guys to notice my value. I even stopped waiting around to be noticed. I traded my title of "Lady in Waiting" for my crown of "Lady in Living".

OWN YOUR VALUE

Alright, you *know* your value. You *practice* your value. Now what? OWN it girl! Own your value my sister! After I traded my former title of "lady in waiting" for my crown of "Lady in Living", I started to invest in myself and to add even more value to others, just as CHRIST had called me to do.

Now, let me break down my terminology here. When I say **"Lady in waiting", I use this term, to mean a woman who is waiting around for a man to perceive her value and to validate her.**

This term does <u>not</u> refer to a woman who is waiting for God's best. We definitely <u>should</u> wait on GOD'S best, but meanwhile, live the life that GOD destined for us in purpose and destiny (be a lady in Living).

So, I upgraded my former title of "Lady in Waiting" to "Lady in Living". I stopped waiting for a man to "validate" my value and *I chose myself!* I began to pursue the real journey of becoming a content single in CHRIST and self. Even a step further, I began the journey to becoming a "Lady in Pursuit"- A lady in pursuit of God's heart and presence and also my purpose in CHRIST. I choose myself as an investment in The Kingdom. Matthew 6:33 tells us "seek ye first the Kingdom of GOD and His righteousness, and all else will be unto you". As we seek JESUS first, we can be confident that in GOD's timing, He will send us a mate. Even if we never get married, we should be content and whole in CHRIST and as a woman of God.

However, the purpose of this book is not so much focused on motivating you to wait on a mate or a job or career, etc. Instead, I aim to encourage you to seek happiness and self-fulfillment in CHRIST and live a righteous life that is filled with God's purpose, as you choose yourself and CHRIST in the process. The rest will come in its timing 😌

Don't wait for a man or certain career, or certain group of friends...etc, for your life to "start". Choose to invest in yourself today and live a life, according to GOD'S Will and purpose and watch fulfillment come!

Don't use purpose and destiny as a "bargaining chip" with JESUS to say that you will live for CHRIST so that you can get what you want-just as a side bar there). Actually become a "Lady in Living" and a "Lady in Pursuit" of God. Seek His heart, not His hand, and He will give you what is in His hand, just because you sincerely seek His heart first and foremost.

Although, you have just read many pages on relationships, I want you to know that this book is not just about relationships. This book is about having a core sense of value that will then emanate and spring forth into all areas of your life: personal relationships, career, health, etc. When you know, practice, and own your own value, you will have better quality relationships, better quality health, better value in your career, calling and purpose, etc. Since you know your value, you practice your value. You now own your value.

How would this look like for you in a career? You've put in tons of applications with no call backs or maybe a few rejection letters; meanwhile, you have Divine vision, purpose, and passion brewing within you. Own your own value instead of waiting for another employer to view, accept or determine your value to them. Own your own value and invest in yourself.

Start that ministry that God is calling you to do. Start and build that business that God gave you vision for. If you need more vision, pray for it. Ask and ye shall receive. Seek, ye shall find. Knock, and the door shall be opened to you.

How would this look like for you in health? Instead of you waiting for someone else to tell you that you are more attractive to him when you exercise or look a certain weight, choose yourself first. Choose to love your body and have great health, not because you want a desired outcome based on what a man desires of you. Instead, choose to implement a healthy lifestyle because your body is the Holy Temple of the Lord and you are worth taking care of yourself. The outer results will just be "icing on the cake" after that. Choose to exercise and eat healthy based on your true God given value that says that your body is indeed, the very same Temple that our good Heavenly Father resides and indwells.

Remember that Mercedes that we talked about earlier? That Mercedes has value that everyone perceives. We talked about when the Mercedes is sold door to door, its perceived value is diminished. Well, that was more so about knowing and practicing the value. Follow me with this example to illustrate *ownership* of the "Mercedes".

If you went out and purchased a Mercedes with a down payment and now had a car note, you still do not own the value that car. The dealership or the bank owns it, until you pay the full amount. You have entered into a contract with the bank of the dealership to pay the full amount. They can repossess the value of that car at any point that you fail to make a payment. It is "yours" as long as they say it is yours. Christ paid the full amount for your life. He owns the deeds to your worth and He freely gives it to you.

You see, when you rent your value, just as with the rented Mercedes, which requires a payment to retain its value with you, you have to give payment in relationships and other areas when you rent yourself out. In relationships or careers perhaps, there's always a point of payment in order to receive "value". In a relationship where you rent your value, your payment may come in the form of providing sexual favors to a man in order for him to tell you how good you are (at the risk of your true value within.) Or maybe your "payment" is accepting or succumbing to insults, abuse, or manipulation, in order to retain the man's good "favor", as he tells you he loves you, but beats you and cheats on you. The list goes on. As an employee with rented value, your payment may come in the form of accepting way less pay for the value that you know that you add, or maybe some other payment, etc.

Now, when you purchase that same Mercedes in full, with no remaining balance, you walk out as the owner of that Mercedes, and now own the full value of the Mercedes.

This same analogy is true when you allow society or other people to determine your worth. You are simply "renting" your own value and allowing other to diminish your value at any time. How does this play out in real life? Let's look at it from several perspectives and roles. (Two examples: as an employee and as a mate in a relationship):

Employee Scenario:

You are a hard worker and show up to work on time most of the times. You always show up seeking to add value to your employer; you contribute a lot to your boss, your coworkers and every one of the customers or clients. Yet, you are unacknowledged and you work long hours for little pay. You have to work with coworkers or colleagues who don't offer half the value you add (this is not to compare yourself or for you to feel superior to anyone). You begin to realize that the work that you do is under met with due payment and your boss shows no appreciation. As a result, you begin to offer less value of yourself and your work ethic drops.

You say "why even try? My co-workers do even less than me and are getting paid the same, so I will give mediocre effort since excellence is not valued nor met by others". Does this sound familiar?

What you've actually done is diminished your own value added because you did not receive external validation from your employer or others. Do you see how you have allowed someone else to determine the value you bring? If you are going to be excellent, be excellent, whether someone pats you on the back or not.

I've told myself the same things before and had the same experiences, but God convicted (not condemned) me. He lovingly showed me that my employer does not determine my value, regardless of how much he or she pays me. If money were a true standard of how much I am worth, then truly, there would be no amount sufficient enough to portray my true value, because I am that valuable and so are you. Money cannot buy our value my sister. Christ paid that cost with His life, which was the full payment that give us full value (inherent value). God brought me through an entire season where He taught me to bring value and to be excellent, regardless of how my coworkers worked or did not work; regardless of my pay, or what I would gain. God taught me to work, even in all areas of my life, with such a true Spirit of Excellence. What does this look like?

Here's a real-life example: I worked at a salad place where my primary job was to greet customers and to maintain the cleanliness of the salad bar. Instead of me complaining about how that job was beneath my "professional status" and education (which was initially a temptation), I chose to submit to God and my employer, at that time, and to add real value. Now, granted, I am NOT saying that you should just settle for any job and then submit out of settling. I am NOT saying that you should not seek a job or career that is in line with your professional training and experience. What I AM saying is that for me, those were the circumstances at that time. I was working at the salad place, WHILE, I was working toward something greater, after just having had been laid off from a prior professional job. Instead of me complaining and giving mediocre effort, I chose to make the best of it and actually serve those around me, while I still pursued plans of elevation. I worked as though I worked unto the Lord and not unto man. Colossians 3:23 says, "Work willingly at whatever you do, as though you were working for the Lord rather than for people." (NLT)

I let my work be a form of worship to Jesus. I made my job my mission field. I sought to add value to every customer that came through those doors and added value to them as I ministered to them; God honored this act of worship. I could have allowed my employer at the time to determine the value that I gave by saying, "well, since you are only paying me 'x' amount of dollars, I'm only going to give you 'this much' value. Instead, I gave all the value I had and it planted good seeds, which yielded good crop else where. You reap what you sow. Do not be deceived: Galatians 6: 7-8 says, "God cannot be mocked. A man reaps what he sows. [8] Whoever sows to please their flesh, from the flesh will reap destruction; whoever sows to please the Spirit, from the Spirit will reap eternal life. " (NIV). You may sow in one field, but reap in another.

What would have happened, if instead of choosing to flow in the Spirit, I chose to operate out of my flesh and did not do any work of any value, but simply showed up to collect a paycheck? One, that would have reflected poorly on my Father, who I professed very boldly and unapologetically. Secondly, that would have reflected poorly on myself. How different would I have been if I had conformed to the ways of the world and worked with mediocrity and apathy as most of the workers did? We as Christians are called to stand out and be set apart, even from the way we labor in the field, regardless of where that field is.

So, this is my point: I did not "rent" the Mercedes as in our first example. I "bought" the Mercedes, because I held the keys and it was my name on the title, not my employer's. I did not allow my employer to determine the value that I brought. I determined the value that I had and brought, because I own my value, not my employer. I also did not look at my value through the eyes of my employer, as in his eyes, I was only worth a little more that minimum wage. I saw my value, even as an employee, through the eyes of God and conducted myself as such.

Here is the take away about value and employers. You have the power in regards to how much an employer pays you. You can negotiate that salary based on what you bring to the table. Even more so, please know your value in that you do not have to accept any old job that pays you less than what you are worth. (though no monetary value truly encapsulates your whole value). You choose what you want to accept and what the employer wants to pay you; if it is not enough, find a job that will pay you what you bring to the table.

Now, I understand that sometimes we have to take certain positions in the meantime, just to pay bills and stay afloat, but this should be only WHILE we are building something greater to get to the next level. We should not settle for crumbs, when we are created as Royalty, meant to sit at our King's table. We are not the dogs that wait under the table for other's left overs. This is in business, relationships, etc..

Maybe you have diminished your value as an employee because you were told that you don't have enough experience or skill, and did not add any real value to the employer. As a result, you have told yourself that you are not valuable and you feel like or have felt like you cannot do anything right. You approach employment as a desperate need, rather than with the value that you actually are worth and bring. Here is what I say to you, my sister; You do have what it takes! You are NOT a failure. You are NOT worthless. You DO have value, even without the experience (it's just in potential form without the experience). You have real worth, regardless!

Relationships

Let's look at an example of renting vs. owing your worth in relationships (romantic-wise)

So, you are in a relationship or maybe you are not in a relationship, per se. Let's look at your interactions with men in the dynamics of a relationship, whether you are officially in one or hoping to be in one.

So, there's this guy that you are interested in. He may or may not reciprocate that interest. So, you "like" this guy. You think he is super cute, handsome, and all that.

You like the butterflies that you feel when you are around him. He makes you blush when you are around him. Your heart beats so fast when you see him. You daydream about him and think about him. You dream about him and think about him when you're not around him. You coordinate "chance" rendezvous to see him, as though you did not know he would be where you planned to be. Am I hitting it right? At this point, you have even planned your wedding to this man and have name all 3-5 of your kids. You have scribbled your name and his name a million times on paper! I have been there too and so has nearly every woman at some point (who cares to admit it).

When you see this man, you find excuses to talk to him. You bat your eyes; you wiggle your hips, and you spend 3 hours trying to pick out an "outfit" that you think will attract this guy. Let's be honest, the outfits that you pick are a lot more "risqué" than you want to admit to yourself. You've done all of this, now what? Maybe the guy "likes" what he sees and asks you out. You get super excited and tell all of your friends how you got him "sprung". You tell your friends, "girl, I know he has been looking at me all this time; he knows he wants me!"

Now, you go on a date with this guy. He tells you what you want to hear. You buy what he is selling. He "seals the deal" after a date or two and in today's culture, you two are "an item". You tell all of your friends, "girl he loves me, I think he is the one."

What just happened in all of this? You've went all in, acting out of emotions and leaving your heart unguarded. Now you are "head over heels" for this guy and his is cool as a cucumber. He now has your heart, and thus, your head. He can tell you anything he wants to and you are a fish on a hook, which he can throw back into the pond, at any point he chooses. This man tells you that you are beautiful and everything he has ever wanted. He tells you that you are "wifey", yet he has no real intention of making you his wife. He has all of the wifey benefits with no real commitment of a ring and marriage.

You see red flags in this guy, but ignore it, because well, you are "wifey" and it's been a dream of yours since forever to be a wife, right? Before long, this man, who used to "wine and dine" you, starts to disrespect you, but you justify it. You say, "oh, it was a misunderstanding". The compliments stop and the insults start; The insults become more frequent. You start to feel the "sting" of his words. Maybe you have even "given yourself" sexually to this man to prove how much you love him, because you think that if you have sex with him, he might just stay, and maybe even treat you better. You feel like you can make him love you because you are a "great lover" in bed.

At this point, you have formed an ungodly soul tie with this man, as God designed sex to be an act of worship between a man and his wife only. Outside of marriage, sex becomes tainted and is bondage. You are now bound to this man as your souls become intertwined. The Bible talks about this as "cleaving". Ephesians 5:31 says, "For this reason a man will leave his father and mother and be united to his wife, and the two will become one flesh." (NIV). Now, you can't bare the thought of life without this man and you justify his hurtful actions and start blaming yourself. You beat yourself up. You start to feel down, discouraged and unempowered. You feel like you have to "take his stuff" because you believe the lie that he has told you so. "No one else would love you that way he loves you, if not at all" is the lie that he has fed you. You have eaten his lies for breakfast, lunch, dinner and desert. Now you are in bondage with no escape in sight.

This may seem extreme to you, or maybe I have just described your exact situation. All too often this happens to women, but no one talks about it. If this is you, please be encouraged to know that there **is** a way of escape and deliverance and it comes through Jesus Christ. He loves you. He knows you and He wants you! (yes, He still wants you, even after all of it).

Let's help you understand what happened in this scenario, as we dive deeper. To help illustrate, I will use names for the sake of clarity. Let's use "Christina" for the woman and "Tim" for the man. From the very beginning Christina had no true sense of her value and worth. So she found it in the wrongful external validation of a man, "Tim" in this case. Tim perceived this weakness in Christina and manipulated her into a "relationship". There Christina was thinking that it was her who manipulated Tim into liking her by the way she dressed and flirted, when it was Tim who exploited her weakness. Christina diminished her own value by downgrading her temple (her body) with her choice of clothing, just to seduce a man. Adding to sexual temptation, Christina was so "gong ho" for a man that she neglected to guard her heart. She allowed the man to "hold the keys" to her Mercedes, as she fluctuated in her emotions with his words. When he complimented her, she felt on top of the world. When he insulted her, she felt bruised and worthless. Christina was on his rollercoaster and had allowed Tim to own her value. Her value only went up when **he** told her so.

God teaches us in His word in proverbs 4:23, "Above all else, guard your heart, because it is the well spring of life." Tim had all this control over Christina, because she failed to guard her heart and let God bring her the right man in the right time.

The above scenario with Christina and Tim is an example of unhealthy relationships where Christina did not know, practice, nor own her value. Now that we have looked at what has happened behind the scenes in the above scenario, let's look at what Christina should have done to protect herself and what a healthy relationship with value looks like. For the next scenario, we will examine Brenda and Clark.

Brenda has a particular guy of interest, Clark, and sees him around. She is tempted to talk to all of her friends about him, but realizes that she needs to have a handle on her emotions first. Her friends would only encourage her emotions and not lead her to protect her heart. So instead, Brenda takes her attraction of Clark to God. She brings her heart and all emotions to JESUS and talks to Him instead. (There is a place for wise council and accountability, but your primary communication should first be between you and God-**given that you have a healthy balance within yourself and you know the voice of God clearly**.) Otherwise, pray about and seek Godly council, NOT worldly advice. You definitely want to also invite in wise council, while discerning spirits).

Brenda has committed to giving her heart to Christ first and foremost. She lets Jesus download her true value within her heart. It's because she has a relationship of intimacy with Christ, and knows her value in Christ, that she is not so easily flattered by Clark's words or compliments. She is properly guarded. Instead of day-dreaming and fantasizing about Clark, Brenda prays for discernment and direction. She *interviews* Clark on their dates and conversations with **intentionality**. She actually judges the fruit that Clark Produces.

Do you see the difference between Christina and Brenda? Take a moment and reflect...which one are you most like? Which route do you tend to take in relationships- Christina's route or Brenda's route?

Brenda focuses more on God, not Clark, or even herself and how she feels. In turn, she is able to stay grounded in truth, not deception. She has clarity and clearly sees any red flags, at which point, she ends communication with Clark. She does so, because she recognizes her own value and she holds the keys to her Mercedes, not Clark. Her emotions do not go up and down with Clark's words and/or actions. Her worth is already determined before Clark enters the picture, so he did not have the power over her to influence her perception of her value. Brenda *owns* her value; Christina did not-she rented her value.

If you find yourself to be more like Christina than Brenda, do not be discouraged. This book is NOT to bash you or make you feel small in any way! It simply seeks to enlighten you of your own perceived value and how you view yourself.

Whether you're like Christina, who rented her value, or you are like Brenda, who owned her value, be encouraged and know that both Brenda AND Christina have value inside (inherent value). The only difference between the two of them is that one woman (Brenda) saw and carried her own value and caused others to see it and carry it too, and the other woman (Christina) who has the same value, failed to see her own value, so she did not carry nor enforce that value with others.

People cannot and will not enforce value that you yourself do not carry for them to handle. On the other hand, when you know, practice, and own your own value- when you carry and enforce your own value, you set the tone for how others will then be expected to handle your value. People will judge and evaluate your value based on what you submit to them by the way you dress, the way you carry yourself, the way you speak, the things you accept and do not accept, etc...

Remember, it's just like the example of one Mercedes being sold door to door, and the other Mercedes standing tall in the showroom. They both have the same content and value on the inside, just different *perceived* value based on how they are displayed or presented.

If you do find yourself like Christina, from the example above, please know that you have been manipulated and sold a lie. You have had seeds of "devalue" planted in your vineyard by society, media, people, ...etc.

Who has told you that you are ugly? Who has lied to you and told you that you are not smart enough? Or that you are fat? Who or what has planted the lie that you are unlovable, insignificant or inadequate???

Who told you those lies that you will never be enough, which left you feeling not valuable and feeling unworthy to the point where you feel that you have to rent your value for acceptance?

My dear love:

You are BEAUTIFUL.

You are ACCEPTED.

You are SIGNIFICANT.

You are a DIAMOND JEWEL.

YOU. ARE. ENOUGH! (Period, no exceptions!)

I want to tell you more about who God says you are and how much value you actually have ownership of and authority. First, please allow me to lead you in a simple prayer:

(Prayer)

"Heavenly Father of my created being: I come to You, broken and disillusioned at the real concept of my true value. I have been sold a lie from the enemy and have mistakenly bought into that deception. I don't know where to begin with unraveling and unpacking this lie that has given birth to chains that I find myself entangled. Please come into my heart, Savior and Father of everything good. Show me your true love and its real meaning. Take hold of my mind and RELEASE me of these lies. Undo the scarring of the past experiences that I have endured, as a result of not walking in my true identity and value. Lead me into all truths and make me whole again.

I declare that I AM FREE of EVERY lie of the enemy! Show me how to see, know, practice, and own my true value within, being anchored in Christ. Thank you for dying for me, as with your death, my *true* value was born.

In the mighty, loving name of JESUS, I pray, Amen.

Chapter Three:

Access the Process

In the last chapter, we talked more about **inherent value.** In this chapter, I will introduce the topic of **value added through the process toward purpose and greatness.** We will also continue to discuss inherent value, as in the last chapter.

My sister, wherever you find yourself with your value-whether you need help with recognizing your true value, or you have a good handle on knowing your value-know that God has a process for you that is designed to help you continually grow in efforts towards manifesting greatness as God intended. You may find yourself in one of the following 3 categories:

1. You don't know your value at all.
2. You know your value, but do not actively practice it.
3. You Know and occasionally practice your value, but you do not own your value.

Regardless of which category you find yourself in, be mindful of, respect, and honor the process of which God is taking you and wants to take you. He knows your heart, your current circumstances, and past experiences that has landed you wherever you are. God also knows your deepest desires for a husband, career, a certain lifestyle, etc. There is a process that you must undergo to be adequately prepared to receive the blessing and to properly handle everything that comes along with it. God wants to take you to a place where you know, practice and own your value in all of these areas and more, so that you can walk in the fullness of the Royal priesthood for which He created you. He wants to prepare you for your inheritance, starting with your identity, self-perception and value at the foundation.

STEPS OF THE PROCESS

Now, my dear sister, realize that your process will look different from my process or someone else's process. Though we may have similarities, know that God ordains and allows a specific process for you and your walk, which matches your unique God-destined calling and purpose. Here are just some key highlights, tips and common steps that may play out differently for different individuals:

Toward the Journey to Owning Your Own Value:

STEP 1: BE REAL WITH YOURSELF

Be real with yourself. Take a self-assessment of where you really are with perception of your self-worth. You either fall into one of the 4 following categories:

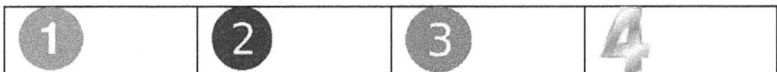

1	2	3	4

Category 1. You don't know your worth at all.

Category 2: You know your worth, but don't Practice or own it.

Category 3: You Know and practice your worth, but do not fully own it. You sometimes transfer ownership of your value to others. ("you rent the Mercedes")

Category 4: You know, practice and successfully OWN your own value. ("you own the Mercedes")

*Pause here at this point, before reading on. Complete the self-assessment worksheet(**at the back of the book, after the epilogue)** to find out which "worth-application" category you fit into from the categories above. Then come back here at this spot and pick up the reading with step 2 below.

STEP 2: ACKNOWLEDGE THE PROCESS

Once you discover your starting point of where you currently are with the above categories, acknowledge that there is a process necessary to get you from where you are to where you need to be, if you are not already in category 4. Even if you are in category 4, there is still more work to do in the maintenance phase.

Once you have acknowledged the truth of where you find yourself with your perception of your worth and how you apply your worth, the next step in acknowledging the process is this: Breathe and have hope for the outcome. Do not get down and out on yourself about how you feel about yourself already, if you do find yourself in any of the first 3 categories. It is ok! You will get to where you need to be, in sticking with the process and keeping Christ at the center. Do not allow the enemy to put any further negative thoughts in your mind and do not allow him to condemn you.

I once found myself somewhere in between category 1 and 2 when I was a young lady in my late teens. I then progressed to category 3 in my early twenties. I have literally walked and progressed through all of these stages, all the way up to stage 4, where I am today. This was done only by the grace of God and the everlasting love and guidance of Christ. Having had grown through these (difficult at times) processes, I want to now help you grow through whatever stage you find yourself.

Do not feel any less than if you do find yourself in any of the first 3 categories. Be encouraged and know that God is faithful to finish the great work in you that He has begun. (Philippians 1:6)

Philippians 1:6 "Being confident of this very thing, that He which has begun a good work in you will perform it until the day of Jesus Christ."

It just takes a process my dear. So, if you lack confidence and are frustrated with how much you lack confidence in yourself (or anything else that you feel you are lacking) take heart and know that it all comes through the process. The confidence comes in knowing, practicing, and owning your value because once you own your value, no one can revoke your ownership or intimidate you.

Therefore, in step 2: "Acknowledge the Process", I encourage you to breathe and have hope. Trust that God is able to do exceedingly and abundantly more than what you could ask or think. (Ephesians 3:20)

Be patient by walking in the Spirit. Galatians 5:22 tells us that one of the fruit of the Spirit is patience. Allow God to perfect you with His supernatural peace and patience, as you undergo the process. Remember that you (and us all) are a work in progress. God is the Master Potter and you, my sister are the clay. God is more than capable of fashioning the clay that is you, in the way that He sees you, not who you are limited to see. God wants to broaden your view of yourself as He shapes you into all that He foreknew you to be. Jeremiah 1:5 says, "Before I formed you in the womb I knew you; before you were born I set you apart.)

Trust God as He shapes you throughout the process. He holds the blueprint and knows what stage of building you are in. He knows what to lay down in your foundation. He knows what your walls look like, what the content of your interior should look like and He is shaping you, even right now. He is strengthening, perfecting, and establishing you. (1 Peter 5). God sometimes shows you your value in showing you just how valuable you are to Him; He loves you and protects you through trials and tribulations, through the fire. God has allowed you to be shaped and purified. Just as precious silver and gold goes through the fire to perfect blemishes and to be purified- thereby increasing value, you too my sister go through the similar process of being refined in the fire.

Take a vase for instance, before a beautiful vase can become a beautiful vase, it is simply raw elements that must come together. Once the vase is shaped by the Potter's desires, the last great step is to place the vase in the fire, so as to proof the vase. This thereby, creates stability for the vase to hold its shape, and its value. You see, if that vase were to prematurely go on the shelf before finishing the process, it would break by the mere handling of the vase coming into contact with so many people touching it. However, if the vase is fully perfected during the process of the fire, it can now *withstand* being handled by so many people and will not break!

If you went into a store on a mission for the perfect vase for decoration in your home, you would seek out the vase at the store. Not only would you want the vase for decoration, but the vase serves 2 purposes:

1. Decoration 2. *Functionality*

Imagine that as you went out to the store in pursuit of the right vase, that you picked up a particular vase and it fell apart! This vase fell apart because it had been prematurely pulled out of the fire and did not complete the process of being perfected in the fire. Would you then pick up the remaining pieces and proceed to check out at the register? Of course not! Why not? You would not make that purchase simply because the vase does not and cannot hold the capacity to fulfill the service of your purpose. It looks good on the outside, but when put to the test, that vase lacked depth and sustainability. It was good on the outside, but it had no substance.

You see, you are just as this vase. God created you to shine for your vase to reflect his goodness with the light of Christ (this is your decoration). The only difference between you and the vase from the example above, is that God intends for you to have substance and value that is only produced from the process of the fire. God created you to serve His purpose in you (this is your functionality-God's Will).

Value is more than what is on the outside. Value is more than beauty. Value is *content* of what is on the *inside*. The process dictates your content (beyond your basic content) and therefore, dictates what goes on the inside of you. This is what makes value. God values what is on the inside of you and has great plans for what you hold inside. Every hurt, every pain, every bitter and traumatic experience, has informed you of how you perceive your value in all areas of your life and self; but these same painful experiences, once you overcome them, build valuable content within as it makes you stronger and therefore useful to the Master. So you see my dear, the process is **essential**. Guard your heart throughout the process and trust that your Master Potter, JESUS, knows what He is doing in you.

You will find such joy and strength as you *grow (not just go)* through the process.

There are 4 major stages of the process. As you start out in the process, your first reaction is to *eject* yourself from the process. As you grow, your next inclination is to *encounter* the process. In the next stage of the process, as you mature, you **embrace** the process. The last stage of the process, with the most maturity, is that you start to *enjoy* the process.

*Stages of Positioning in the Process

(the 4 E's)**

Ejection- In this stage of the process, in immaturity, you make every attempt to eject or remove yourself from the process. You are solely focused on how the process afflicts you and hurts you. You have no real view of the bigger picture. Due to the fact that you are so focused on yourself and how this affects you, you miss what God is trying to do in your life, for your life, and for His purpose.

Encounter- In this stage, you are a bit more mature in your walk and process-you are aware that this hurts and afflicts you, but you make a conscious and *intentional* effort to no longer abort, but to encounter the storm throughout the process. You are aware that God is doing something in you throughout this process. You no longer try to remove yourself from the process and you *accept* what God is doing because you have a glimpse of the bigger picture.

(Note, it is up to you to *discern* whether you are in the fire because God is allowing you to go through it, or if you are really facing demonic attack. That's outside the scope of this book, but just wanted to make you aware since I am using the term "accept" the process. You should never accept demonic attack!)

Embrace- In this stage, you have matured a lot, throughout the process, so when storms come your way, you do not run. You STAND your ground and you embrace the difficulty of the process. You understand that God loves you and that He is working His eternal weight of glory in and through you. You know that what God is doing and building in you has eternal significance and value to the

Kingdom. In this stage, you know that God is not "doing this to you", but rather that He is training you up for your crown of the Queen that He has purposed in you. He is constructing value in you through the fire, which will prepare you to reign and rule in all areas of your life and for the Kingdom. He is raising you up to be the person that He envisioned when He created you and is preparing you for your inheritance.

This is why it is so crucial for you to perceive what God is doing. This is why it is so imperative that you also perceive, receive, and believe the value that God has placed down on the inside of you. God wants to raise you up, but the world, the enemy, society, and certain people continually try to devalue you and tear you down. They work to convince you that you need permission from someone or that you have to wait for someone to give you opportunity based on the value that they see in you. The truth is that God has already settled your core value within you and constantly adds to that value by way of the process.

Enjoy- In this stage, you are the most mature (but always growing) in that you recognize real value of the process. You no longer coward away from trials and tribulations. Jesus tells us in John 16:33, "In this life, you will have trials and tribulations, but be of good cheer, for I have overcome the world."

In this stage, you seek God throughout the process and *listen for instruction* for next steps, even though you are afflicted. You know that God is not doing this to you, but through you and for you, because He loves you. You celebrate the storm because you know that it is producing something in you or it is removing debris from you that would devalue you. Either way, God is creating and harnessing true value within you and real content. He is removing from you, all of the toxic waste that the world has conditioned and deposited on the inside of you.

God is removing and subtracting all of the mess that depreciates your value and that undermines your identity, value, and authority in Him. You recognize the importance of the big picture and you know that all things work together for the good of those who love God and who are called according to God's purpose (Romans 8:28). You can say to yourself, "it was good for me that I have been afflicted, that I might learn thy statutes" (psalm 119:71-KJV)

Regardless of where you find yourself, whether in stage 1, 2, 3, or 4 of the 4 E's, know that God allows pressure to penetrate the olive, so that its oil can flow freely! God is simply increasing your flow of oil, which is your true anointing, content, and value in Him. God is working out your anointing for His purpose, so that you are not just an empty shell that looks good and is decorated. He wants to make sure that you are also filled with, not just content, but the *right content,* and that you are functional-useful to the Master and fit for his good purpose and use. 2 Timothy 2:21 says, "if a man therefore purge himself from these, he shall be a vessel of honor, sanctified, and meet for the Master's use and prepared unto every good work". (KJV)

Once you understand the true value of the process that happens around you and on the inside of you, you are not so apt to give control or access to someone else over your own value. You know what it took to endure the affliction, even when you did not understand. Therefore, you will not allow someone to devalue, nor diminish your value-whether that be romantic relationships, family, friendships, business, work, etc.

STEP 3: ENDURE THE PROCESS:

Trust God throughout the process. Things will get very difficult through certain parts of your process; difficult, yet not impossible. At times, you will want to quit and give up, DON'T QUIT! NEVER QUIT my sister! God will give you *grace* to endure, for His grace abounds much and is never-ending. 2 Corinthians 12:9 tells us that God's grace is sufficient and His strength is made perfect in weakness. Do not try to do it in your own strength, because you will surely fail on your own. You need to continually *fill* up with Holy Spirit. This is the same, for example, as you filling up your car's gas tank with gas. In order for you to be able to operate and drive your car to get you to where you need to be, you need to constantly fill your tank with gas and do regular maintenance to keep it functional. When you stop putting gas and stopping getting regular maintenance, what happens? Your car, which has the potential to get you somewhere, becomes stagnant until you fill it with more gas and keep it maintained.

There are times throughout this process where you will be on "E" (empty) and you will need the strength and grace of God's love and Holy Spirit, which will equip you to *endure the process.* The most important thing you have to do in order to successfully endure, is to put on the full armor of God every single day! I'll talk more about this below.

Here are some tools that can help you along the process:

1. Put on the Armor of God <u>every day</u>.
   Did she say every day?! YES! I guarantee you, the day that you feel like it's ok to skip out on putting on your armor, that is the day you will feel the enemy's attack the hardest. Make no mistake, we are in a war composed of battle after battle- granted you have to know which battles to fight, how and when. Without the Armor of God, you leave yourself completely defenseless against the enemy's attack. You leave room for yourself to be put into a position of a victim, when God has clearly given you the tools to be the VICTOR.

   The Armor of God is found in Ephesians 6:10-18.

   I will take you through each part of the Armor that comprises your soldier gear of protection against the enemy. This is essentially important for your process.

   First, let's look at the scripture:

   Ephesians 6:10," Finally, be strong in the Lord and in His mighty power. (verse 11) put on the full armor of God, so that you can take your stand against the devil's schemes. (verse 12) For our struggle is not against flesh and blood, but against the authorities, against the powers of this dark world and against the spiritual forces of evil in the heavenly realms. (verse 13) Therefore, put on the full armor of God, so that when the day of evil comes, you may be able to stand your ground, and after you have done everything to stand (verse 14) stand firm then, with the (armor of God): 1. ***belt of truth*** buckled around your waist, with the 2. ***Breastplate of righteousness*** in place (verse 15) and your feet fitted with readiness that comes from the 3.***gospel of peace****, (verse 16) In addition to all this, take up the **4. Shield of faith** , with which you can extinguish all the flaming arrows of the evil one. (verse 17) Take the **5. Helmet of salvation** and the **6. Sword of the Spirit,** which is the word of God. (verse 18) And pray in the Spirit on all occasions with all kinds of prayers and requests with this in mind, be alert and always keep on praying for all the Lord's people.

Let's break this down:

1. **Belt of Truth** : The belt of truth represents the truth of God. God teaches us to stay anchored in His truth, as found in His word, so that we do not fall into deception, nor the lies of the world. Romans 12:2 tells us "do not be conformed to the ways of this world, but be ye transformed by the renewing of your mind.

Tip: How to use the Belt of Truth: Compare your beliefs and actions to the truth of God's word in the Bible.

2. **Breastplate of Righteousness** – The breastplate of Righteousness means being honest, good, humble, and fair to others. It is great to note the position of the breastplate. It covers and protects your heart and other vital organs. God tells us in Proverbs 4:23, "Above all else, guard your heart, for it is the wellspring of life".

The heart is the primary line of communication between you and God. All of this is a part of worship, as you commune with the Father in your heart. Scripture says, "Behold, I stand at the door, and knock: if any man hear my voice, and open the door, I will come in to him, and will sup (dine) with him, and he with me." (KJV)

3. **Shoes of the Gospel of Peace-**This means that you continually take up and walk in the peace of God, especially during trials and adverse times. Jesus said in John 14:27, "Peace I leave with you; my peace I give you. I do not give as the world gives. Do not let your heart be troubled; and do not be afraid."

4. **Shield of Faith-** Your shield of faith is your hope in God. This is trusting that God will do exactly what He has promised. He is not a man that He should lie. Psalm 118:8 says, "It is better to trust in God, than to put confidence in man. (This includes your own self/flesh, because God knows best!) This scripture is not saying that you cannot trust anyone. It is saying that it is more wise to trust in the wisdom of God, than the sound

facts and thoughts of mere man, which includes yourself. God sees the whole picture from beginning to the end and everything in between. Faith requires trusting God for what you do not see or even understand. God's ways are higher than your ways and His thoughts are higher than your thoughts. Trust God's guidance over your own thoughts.

Hebrews 11:1 tells us, "Faith is the substance of all things hoped for, the evidence of things not seen. Romans 8:24-25 says, "For in this hope we were saved. But hope that is seen is no hope at all. Who hopes for what they already have? (25) But if we hope for what we do not yet have, we wait for it patiently." (NIV)

The Shield of Faith helps keep you anchored in what you are hoping for. It protects you against doubting. God tells us in James 1:6-8, "But when you ask, you must believe and not doubt, because the one who doubts is like a wave of the sea, blown and tossed by the wind. 7 That person should not expect to receive anything from the Lord. 8 Such a person is double-minded and unstable in all they do." (NIV)
God says, do not ask because you surely will not get it when you ask half-heartedly.

I say all of that to say this: the shield of faith is essential during the process, for which God has given you promises for promotion and has given you vision. God will always make provision for the vision! Faith helps get you through the tough times, in believing that God will bring the people, the resources, the location, …etc, for the vision that He has placed within you.

Also, in romantic relationships, for example, faith is essential in believing that God will bring you your spouse who is worthy of your value, instead of you choosing to settle, all because you see no evidence of God bringing anyone. Faith is trusting and believing that God knows what He is doing in and through you and that He has you *exactly* where He needs you, when you are in His Will. God makes No mistakes. Trust God. Trust the process.

5. **Helmet of Salvation-** The Helmet of Salvation means that you put on the mind of Christ, instead of perpetuating carnal thinking. You should contemplate and meditate on spiritually eternal things, rather than worldly things. God tells us in Philippians 4:8, "Whatever is lovely, whatever is admirable, if anything is excellent or praiseworthy, think about such things." Having the Helmet of Salvation means thinking the thoughts that God and Heaven thinks about you. It's about changing your entire mindset to a Heavenly mindset of Royalty and adopting the thought process of God and Heaven.

The enemy will always come to you and try to fill your mind with doubt and discouragement to get you to think that God does not love or care for you. The enemy will also try to get your mind focused on sin, in order to make you feel condemned. He would also try to get your mind on thoughts that lead to sin. The enemy comes to steal, kill, and destroy. He tries to plant thoughts in your mind that devalue you and that is in direct opposition to the true thoughts of God. The more you focus on those thoughts, the more those lies become your reality.

Either way, God tells us to be armed with the mind of Christ and not to entertain, nor dwell on ungodly thoughts that lead us astray. God tells us for this purpose, in 2 Corinthians 10:3-5," (verse 3) For though we live in the world, we do not wage war as the world does (verse 4) For the weapons of our warfare are not carnal, but mighty through God for the pulling down of strongholds! (verse 5) Casting down imaginations and every high thing that exalts itself against the knowledge of God, and bringing into captivity every thought to the obedience of Christ.

You should also use the Helmet of Salvation for every area of your life. Here are a few subcategories for example:

Purpose- Remind yourself of your purpose that has value. Find scriptures that remind you that you are capable and worthy of the purpose that which God has entrusted you, when the enemy comes to cause you to doubt yourself and your usefulness to God.
Career- Find scripture to remind yourself that God can use your career for His purpose and that you are _qualified_ for your career. You can do all things through Christ who strengthens you!
Relationships- (Romantic and Otherwise): Find scripture to remind yourself of God's

intended purpose for every relationship that God has ordained and allowed you to have. Remind yourself that God says that you deserve to have healthy Christian, biblical relationships with Christ at the center. This is for when the enemy comes and tries to tell you that you do not deserve healthy relationships. Relationships have value and serve purpose. Ask God to show you how to properly operate in those God ordained relationships by meditation on the truth in God's word.

6. **The Sword of The Spirit-** The Sword of the Spirit is the Word of God. This is similar to the Helmet of Salvation, in that you meditate on God's truth as found in His word. The Helmet of Salvation is the process and lifestyle of meditating on the word, while the Sword of the Spirit is the literal Word of God itself that is used as a sword to fend against the fiery darts of the enemy. Using the Sword of the Spirit prevents satan's words, which are lies, from being planted. It also is used to uproot existing lies that the enemy was able to plant.

Before you can meditate on the Word of God, you must first fill yourself with the word. You have to read it, know it, meditate on it, and marinate in it, as you become one with the word; it becomes a part of you and you become a part of it. The Sword of the Spirit is what you use when the enemy comes at you with discouragement and lies such as "you're not pretty enough" for an example. God's Word says in Psalm 139:14, "you are fearfully and wonderfully made." In order for you to cut down the lie that you are not beautiful or not enough, you have to know that Word of God to combat those lies. If you do not know specific scriptures, pray and ask God to lead you to some.

The Sword of the Spirit works against all and any lie that the enemy would throw at you in any area of your life. For any and every lie of the enemy, GOD has a Word of Truth to uproot and cut down that lie!

Remember, it is essential for you to go through the valuable process, which builds the content and also equips you for what God created you for. In order to *endure the process*, which can get very difficult, you have to first and foremost, put on the Armor of God every single day! This is your protection and God's **strategy** for you to prevail against the enemy.

Endure the fight like a good soldier. Know that you are not in the battle alone, but that God goes before you and is with you. He has His Angels surrounding you. God is the Commander in Chief and you are a soldier in the army of the Lord. FIGHT WELL. FINISH STRONG. WIN VICTORIOUSLY!

Chapter 4:
Honor the Process/
Honor the Way

When You Want to Give Up

My sister, there will be times when the road gets so difficult, and everything in you will want to give up. There is especially difficulty in the process of coming to own your own value. Throughout life, you may have been told that you were not good enough, or not pretty enough. You've been told that you are too fat, too skinny, or too 'this' or too 'that'. As a result, your own self perception of your own worth, has been diminished. Maybe you have tried to tell yourself differently, but somewhere in your mind, all of those past lies come back to haunt you. You may have made some progress along the process, but those ghosts of the past put you in a tail spin and cause you to regress; not to mention, the process of life that prepares you for your purpose, which has value, has been rough too. I know there have been many times where I wanted to quit and give up. I got tired of going through the motions of "being ok", only to be knocked down again.

It was once a real struggle for me to know my value, as a person, let alone, as a valuable member of Christ's body who had purpose. I went through so many trials, as we all do. I remember vividly the toughest of many trials, where I reached a breaking point. I felt that I just could not go on; I so desperately wanted to give up, but God would not let me. You see, even though I had gotten to a point where I no longer saw value in my life, God spoke to me from His perspective of value of which He was instilling within me throughout the process.

God had made an investment in me and He was not about to let His investment return void! (He has also made an investment in you!). My soul had grown so weary of so many things, of everything that was going on. Although I know in my Spirit, that God was shaping me, my soul was vulnerable to defeat. I had tried and tried. I got back up so many times, only to be knocked down again. Each time, getting up was harder than the last, until one day, I cried out to God, out of sheer desperation. I knew I had a huge calling on my life. I knew God would use me for His Glory, but though my spirit was willing, my soul was weak. I clung to God with every fiber of my being as I sought to fight for my life. I sought to fight for the value and anointing that God was building within me. I was so ready to quit. I had lost my will to live. I wanted to give up, but my God! Thank you Jesus! Then God, in the midst of my former darkness, spoke in a still, gentle voice. He told me if I would only hold on a little longer, then He would bless me more than what I could imagine. He had plans for me. He would not see me perish.

There was so much more that God spoke to me. He spoke life into me as I cried out to Him. The very next day, my life changed forever, as I would ever know it. Little did I know that it would be the beginning of not only a new chapter, but an entire new life! It came gradually, step by step, but that one day set the course and changed the entire course of my life. I would not be sitting here writing this book, if it had not been for The Lord, who graced me with His supernatural strength and peace.

Although I wanted to quit, my soul refused to die. God refused to let me die. He truly comforted me in the midst of it all. So, my sister wherever you find yourself in your process, just know it is essential. God will never leave nor forsake you! Your latter will be greater than you former! God is not finished with you yet. He has plans for you and

He is with you. There is purpose in all of your pain. It will not return unto you void. Your tears are simply an investment that will yield a greater crop in purpose and even destiny. There is value in your process!

There is even value in your pain. Although you may not understand, it may appear rough now, but God is getting ready to cash you a check that will more than return your deposit and investment. *Don't you quit! Don't you slack! Don't you give in!* Don't stop improving yourself, just because others don't see your value. Keep improving yourself and your skills; keep learning and keep investing in your personal and professional development. Keep marching forward proudly (not pridefully) into your destiny! Don't let relationships with certain people derail your emotions and make you want to give up on love nor life, or even on yourself. Don't abort your purpose and destiny!

If you don't invest in yourself, who will? Keep trusting in God; keep showing up to the "rehearsal" during the process-the process of loving yourself, the process of valuing yourself, the process of your process, etc. Keep striving and walking toward and in greatness for the glory of God! He has not brought you this far, only to leave you. God tells you in His word that He will never leave nor forsake you (Joshua 1:5). He is the same yesterday, today, and forevermore (Hebrew 13:8). He knew you before He formed you in your mother's belly (Jeremiah 1:5) and before you knew yourself. He is the Alpha and Omega, the First and the Last, the Beginning and the End; He who was, He who is, and He who is to come (Revelation 1:8, Revelation 22:13). He knows *where* you are, *who* you are, and *how* you are! Guess what, He still loves you! He knows what direction to take you in. He knows how to lead you. So, **don't stop! Don't quit! Don't relent!**

I know it gets hard. I know it gets tough and seems impossible, but remember baby girl, what is impossible with men, *is possible* with God! (Luke 18:27)

You are not God's first project. You are not His first work or art. He knows how to rearrange your pieces to make the masterpiece. He makes *no mistakes* and never leaves you undone. He charges His elect to be great! Don't let anything nor anyone stop you-not even yourself! God wants to restore you, whenever you are in your process. God is faithful to restore. I once was so broken, lost and confused, but glory to God. He loved me backed together again. Every broken and shattered piece, pieces of me that I thought were gone forever, God revived from the dead and brought to new life. God restored what was broken - even better than before! He gave me a new heart, a new mind, a new life, and a greater understanding of His purpose in me. Now, I am walking in exactly who God created me to be! I see why the painful process was essential; It built me. It strengthened me. It prepared me for destiny.

I am so glad that I did not give up. I kept pressing into GOD, even when it hurt like hell and even when I felt I could take no more and that I could not go any longer. It's true what God's word says in Isaiah 40:31, "But they that wait upon the LORD shall renew their strength; they shall mount up with wings as eagles; they shall run, and not be weary; and they shall walk, and not faint". So, wait my sister, on The Lord. Wait also in The Lord, as you rest in Him during your process (and even so during the good times, rest in God).

It may not all make sense now, but trust God; you are worth the process and your process is worth the pain. The pain and sorrow that you feel now cannot compare to the Joy that's coming! Psalm 30:5 says, "Weeping may endure but for a moment, but JOY comes in the morning!" Keep fighting the good fight! Keep telling yourself that you are beautiful, when the enemy lies and tells you that you are not beautiful.

Keep telling yourself that you are competent and capable, when the enemy lies and says that you cannot do anything right. Invest in yourself and build your skills to build your competence.

Keep investing in your personal and professional growth when the enemy lies and tells you that you are wasting your time.

Keep loving yourself and others, when the enemy lies and tells you that there is no such thing as love or that no one will love you.

Keep on my sister, FIGHT, FIGHT for your value!

FIGHT for your sanity and peace of mind!

FIGHT for your TERRITORY!

FIGHT! FIGHT! FIGHT!!!!!!!!!!!!!!!!!!!!!!!!

Don't just lay down and let the devil steal your stuff! Don't let the enemy steal your joy during your process!

YOU BETTER WORK THAT PROCESS GIRL! DON'T LET IT WORK YOU!!!!!

Love yourself by first loving God, who is love. Stay connected and close to the Vine that is JESUS CHRIST and watch GOD pull you out of darkness and into His marvelous light! He is able! He is worthy! He wants to help you; He wants you to take the necessary steps. Walk by faith and not by sight! Remember, there is greatness within you and God is investing and building value in you!

God Has the Blueprint

Darling sister, I know that at times, life feels like a never-ending maze filled with regret, lose, and confusion; you feel like your world is spinning out of control and you do not know which steps to take, right? I've been there too. I remember a time in my life where I felt totally lost and confused. I was so cluttered on the inside, appearing "normal" on the outside, while screaming on the inside for someone to take my hand and lead me in the right way. Have you ever felt that way?

I'm sure you can relate. Throughout the course of my journey, God has helped me to realize that He has it all under control. He has the blueprint! He is the Master Potter that molds the clay that is me and you! He is the Senior Architect that holds the design to what He is building in you. With any plan and design for any big project, such as a house, it is built piece by piece and section by section, to make the whole house. God also is building *you* part by part, season by season, even hurt by hurt. You may not understand why certain things work out the way they do; you wrack your brain, day in and day out, trying to figure out where all the pieces fit or if they fit at all.

I've been there too! God stilled my soul as He told me that His ways are higher than my ways and that His thoughts are higher than my thoughts! So, I will tell you the same thing my dear: God's ways and His thoughts are higher than yours. We cannot always comprehend with our human mind, the great things that God has for us and wants to work through us. Only God is all omniscient and knows all. The great news is that you are I are connected to the very life line that is JESUS CHRIST! He knows all-so anything we need to know, as long as we remain in Him, He feeds it to us through His Holy Spirit. He may not give you the whole picture at once. Sometimes, He will give you the whole picture for a season; other times, He will give you just enough to complete one step. Then step by step, you make the journey.

We are never alone. God steps with us every step of the way. So, do not despair if you do not have all the steps or plan figured out. You are in good hands-God's hands- and no man can pluck you from out of your Father's hands. It is a sure hand that will keep you through the process. When uncertainty comes in and tries to overwhelm you, remember that you are here, not by accident but by *design.* You were pre-destined by God for special works that God, Himself, drew out the very framework of your design, uniquely and specifically to your calling and purpose. Remember, the process builds value-your content and character.

Don't deprive the world, God, nor yourself of knowing the *full* version of who you were *destined* to be. Don't abandon the process for comfort. It is uncomfortable throughout parts of the process, but rest assured that God knows exactly where you are. He knew that you would be where you are. Where you are is no accident. It was either God ordained or God-allowed. Either way, God has *good* intentions towards you and will use all things (good and bad) for your good. Romans 8:28 says, "All things work together for the good of those who love the Lord and are called according to His purpose." Trust God throughout the process. Press into His presence and let Him lead you into all truth, into victory, and into your *destiny*! You may not be able to see the whole picture now, but before you know it, your "house" will be built-room by room and overflowing with great value and joy!

Just as a physical house is constructed from raw elements to make something great which houses and provides shelter, God is going to use your process to build something even greater in you; you will then become the shelter for someone else who is going through the same thing that you went through. By the same spirit of God that comforted you, you will then comfort others through that same Holy Spirit. 2 Corinthians 1:4 says, "By the same spirit of God that comforted you, you will then comfort others through that same Holy Spirit."

Rest in God. Have faith and trust that God knows what He is doing. Remember, you are not His first nor last Project. God is sovereign and He holds the blueprint to all things pertaining to you and more. **Let God be God** and *rest*, knowing that your path is already *strategically* laid out and God makes no mistakes!

Worship through warfare

Worship is both an act and an attitude. True worship is done in spirit and in truth. John 4:23-24 says, [23] Yet a time is coming and has now come when the true worshipers will worship the Father in the Spirit and in truth, for they are the kind of worshipers the Father seeks. [24] God is spirit, and His worshipers must worship in the Spirit and in truth." (NIV)

Worship is more than lip service where you sing songs in church, but God is far from your heart. When you sing songs of true worship, you are tapping into a sacred and intimate place where only you and God reside-where you are one with the Father and He is one with you. You regularly and consistently commune with JESUS and Holy Spirit. God tells us in 1 Samuel 15:16, "man sees the outward appearance, but God sees the heart." He knows exactly what is within your heart.

When I think of worship, I think of communion and fellowship. It is an eternal and internal act and expression of receiving God's love and then expressing that love to God and others. Worshipping Jesus is what air is to our lungs or what our heartbeats are to our body. You cannot survive without air, nor can you live once your heart stops beating. To worship Jesus is to live and to live is to worship Jesus. Worship is the flow of the Spirit in exchange of brokenness for grace and life. Worship is the line of communication and the vine that connects us to the Father. Without worship, we die spiritually, and sometimes, can lead to physical death in many cases. (That's a whole other topic there). Worship is essential in the life of every believer and without the oxygen of worship, we suffocate from life's trials and tribulations; we die in the process.

In this book, I will cover how to worship trough the warfare you face as a part of the process. You will face many types of warfare, including spiritual warfare!

Here are some helpful tools you can use against the warfare that you experience during the process:

First, you must recognize that there are 2 main types of warfare:

1. Natural Warfare
2. Supernatural Warfare

You have to know what you are facing before you know which tools to use. In other words, you have to know the source of diagnosis before you can know what "medicine" to use to combat.

<u>Natural Warfare:</u>

Natural warfare is the after effect of what is already happening in the spiritual realm. Think of this analogy:

Let's take, for example, someone who experiences Grand Mal Seizures. In the natural, we can see the person shaking and convulsing, and sometimes falling to the floor. We can see the person convulsing or falling with our natural eye. However, before it manifested on the outside, something happened on the inside where we could not see what was happening. On the inside of that person's body, action potentials and nerve impulses were firing like crazy (misfiring). Although we cannot see what is happening inside that person's body, we clearly see the after effect on the outside. The root cause was on the inside. The after effect was on the outside.

This same thing applies when talking about natural warfare and spiritual warfare. Although there are some natural circumstances that are simply an outcome of our own choices and doings, there are also natural occurrences that occur as a direct result of what is happening in the spiritual realm. The natural problems and tribulations that you face are simply an outward, natural manifestation of an inward spiritual occurrence.

So, once you know the cause in the spirit, you can manage the effect in the natural, in many cases. Some things are easier than others and certain things take a longer process than others.

How do you do this? You identify what is happening in your natural circumstances, by being aware of what is happening spiritually. In order to be aware spiritually, you have to stay connected to the Vine, who is JESUS CHRIST, and be sensitive to Holy Spirit. John 15:5 says, "you are the branch and I am the Vine. If you remain in me and I in you, you will produce much fruit, but without me, you can do nothing." One way to stay connected to the Vine is to continually be in a mindset, heart and lifestyle of worship. There have been many times where I was facing the most difficult circumstances in the natural, and through worship, God revealed the spiritual source and gave me supernatural strategy and equipment against the struggle (and enemy) during my process. Not to mention, God gave me so much rest in the midst of chaos around me.

Mindset. Heart. Lifestyle.

Throughout your life, you will be faced with (or have been faced with) people who try to tell you who you are and what you are worth. These people try to devalue you and try to diminish your own thoughts and feelings about your worth and value. The enemy will also come along and try to provoke you to things that devalue your content. How does this look? This can play out several ways. Let's visit some scenarios:

Mindset.

1. <u>The enemy or people attack your worth:</u>
   Perhaps someone verbally assaults you with rude, mean and negative insults about how ugly or fat you are; or maybe they tell you that you are incompetent. This is a type of warfare that seems light enough in the natural, but has an evil spirit of condemnation and accusation. You can worship through this warfare by first, NOT receiving that spirit or insult. Do not allow that seed to be planted.

   You can worship God and honor Him in your thoughts by meditating on positive reinforcement in scripture, and meditating on the love of God in your heart, instead of choosing to be affected by what was thrown at you. The enemy would love nothing more than for you to receive those false accusations and lies to get you to view yourself in a negative mindset and view. When you do not see yourself as GOD sees you, you give power to people and the enemy to devalue you.

Heart.

2. <u>The enemy or people attack your character:</u> Remember earlier, in the chapter "Access the Process", we talked about content? Well, a part of your content is what makes up your character. Though we are not perfect, it is God's Will for us to be more like Him in character, since we were created after their image (Father, Son, Holy Spirit). The enemy loves nothing more than to devalue your character and to destroy your witness with others. Let's say, someone initially starts an argument with you or tries their hardest to "push your buttons"; they make every attempt to devalue you by making you go down to their level. What is behind this attack which appears to simply be abrasive attacks in the natural, is really the spirit of offense. The enemy will always try to cause you to receive this spirit because he knows that when you allow yourself to be offended, you operate in the flesh and are no longer walking in the Spirit.

Have you ever had an argument with someone and afterward felt foolish for stooping to their level? In the heat of an argument, you may say things that are not godly. God tells us in His word, that the tongue defiles the whole temple-your body is that Temple. Do you see how the enemy just used someone to cause you to devalue yourself and bring you down passed the level of your real value?

You can worship through this type of warfare by studying the character of God, as found in His Word. You also learn God's character, simply by having an intimate relationship with Him through JESUS CHRIST. Once you know God's character, you emulate it. We are to be as God and Christ, as we were made in His image. So, the next time that someone intentionally attempts to tempt you into devaluing yourself by provoking an ungodly reaction out of you, do yourself and God a favor! Choose to *retain* your value in CHRIST. Remain in the godliness of our Savior, instead of giving into who and how others try to define you to be.

Lifestyle.

3. The enemy or people try to attack your lifestyle: Remember, a main part of worship is lifestyle. The enemy would love nothing more than to tempt you to live a lifestyle that does not reflect CHRIST or who God has called you to be. This type of warfare can come in varying degrees and scenarios. Some examples of ungodly lifestyle are: excessive drinking, having sex outside of marriage, envies, witchcraft, a deceitful tongue, adultery,... etc.

Galatians 5:19-21 says this:

"Now the works of the flesh are manifest, which are these; adultery, fornication, uncleanness, lasciviousness, idolatry, witchcraft, hatred, variance, emulations, wrath, strife, seditions, heresies, envying, murders, drunkenness, reveling, and such like these: of which I tell you as I have told you in times past, that they will not inherit the Kingdom of God".

Opposite of these works of the flesh are the works of The Spirit (of God-Holy Spirit), which are found in Galatians 5:22-23, [22] "But the fruit of the Spirit is love, joy, peace, longsuffering (patience), kindness, goodness, faithfulness, [23] gentleness and self-control. Against such things there is no law." (NKJV)

When you walk in the flesh, you produce things of the flesh, which decreases the value of what God intended for you. When you walk in the Spirit, you produce the fruit of The Spirit, which is parallel to all that is valuable in Christ. Make no mistake, **I am not saying that when you sin, you are no longer valuable.** *I am saying that when we sin, we diminish the value of what God put in us and what He intended for us.* With sin, we tarnish what is pure and holy, as we give place to what is dirty.

So, instead of giving into temptation, let us walk in the Spirit and *produce* what is valuable to God and His Kingdom. "I say then: Walk in the Spirit, and you shall not fulfill the lust of the flesh.". (Galatians 5:16-NKJV). The NLT version of the Bible puts it this way: "So I say, let the Holy Spirit guide your lives. Then you won't be doing what your sinful nature craves."

4. <u>The enemy or people tries to attack your attitude:</u> The enemy will always come alongside of you to tempt you into focusing on everything that is going wrong in your life. He aims to get you to become frustrated and bitter, which leads you to complain about everything. You no longer focus on what God <u>has</u> given you, but become obsessed with what God has not given you and what you don't have. Your attitude becomes toxic, as you become ungrateful for all that God has already done for

you. Have you ever heard the expression, "your attitude determines your altitude"? This is actually biblical. Matthew 23:12 states, "but those who exalt themselves will be humbled, and those who humble themselves will be exalted".

I love how Joyce Meyers always says, "complain and remain, or praise and be raised" (Joyce Meyer)

If you continue to complain about how things are and what you don't have, why would God give you more? If you make it all about you, that is simply selfish. God tells us, we must decrease, so that HE can increase.

Yet, if you remain humble and adopt a Spirit of Gratitude and maintain a positive attitude, God will bless you with increase. Luke 16:10 says, "but he that is faithful in that which is least, is faithful also in much, and whoever is unjust in the least is unjust also in much. You should also know that God says that to much is given, much is required, so know that the thing that you are praying for in increase, comes with responsibility and you have to undergo a process to be prepared to handle such a big responsibility. God will always test you with little, before He gives you more.

Remember, earlier in the chapter of "Access the Process", we talked about your content that is developed via the process and how God then uses, for His Kingdom, what He has developed in you. Another type of warfare that you will experience at times is what appears in the natural, as disorganization, clutter, confusion, and laziness. This is due to, what in the spiritual realm, is really the spirit of confusion and disorder. There is also a spirit of procrastination, the spirit of python,...etc.

God tells us in His Word, "Let all things be done decently and in order" (1 Corinthians 14:40- KJV). God is not the author of confusion, but the Prince of Peace! "For God is not the author of confusion, but of peace, as in all churches of the saints" (1 Corinthian 14:33 KJV).

The enemy loves to try to keep you in a state of disorder, confusion and clutter because he knows that you will be distracted and discouraged, by all of this and so overwhelmed that you will just quit on what God is calling you to do. The enemy wants you to quit the process that prepares you for greatness and that builds God's valuable content in you. The enemy uses the spirit of procrastination and laziness to get you to slack and delay God's plans in and for you. You can combat this type of warfare by worshipping God and by adopting a disciplined lifestyle.

So, you have issues with disorganization; here's what you can do! Study and research simple ways to organize your life, thoughts and actions. (see more details in the workbook that accompanies this book)

So, you feel cluttered, then get to the root cause of what seems to be cluttering you. Is it emotionally rooted and manifesting in all areas of your life?

To combat the spirit of procrastination and laziness, you must adopt a spirit of strict discipline and focus (with much prayer to pave the way). Choose to honor God by living a lifestyle where you are so committed to God and His process that prepares you. Think of it like rehearsal for the big recital. What you choose to do on a daily basis forms your end results. Your success is a matter of what you do on a daily basis as well. So, worship God in your actions. Worship God in your habits, which then turns into a great lifestyle, which honors God's being and great purpose.

Worship God in your daily thoughts, attitude, behavior, actions, …etc. The habits that you form today determine the *death* or *life* of your tomorrow. So make them good, positive and healthy ones which honor God and are Christ-centered. You will be better off for it.

The greatest part of a lifestyle of worship with The Father, is building intimacy through prayer, meditation, and even fasting. Simply having a real conversation with God, instead of reciting vain repetition is all it takes. Let Him in your heart. The closeness that we experience with Christ is the most valuable thing that we have, next to our salvation that He so graciously gave and gives.

Praise for Promotion

There will be many parts throughout your process where you will find yourself increasing in your perception of your value. You will find yourself in a particular position where you feel you are overqualified and have way too much value to offer for what you get in return. Maybe this is a job. Maybe you feel that you are smarter and more capable than your boss and you wonder why you have to submit to him or her. You wonder how and why you are even there; or maybe you find yourself under someone's authority in your church group or organization,...etc.

Remember, God still calls you to honor who He has placed in authority over you and God calls us to submission as we honor those over us. We are to pray for them as well. 1 Timothy 2:1-3 states, "I exhort therefore, that, first of all, supplications, prayers, intercessions, and giving of thanks, be made for all men;

² For kings, and for all that are in authority; that we may lead a quiet and peaceable life in all godliness and honesty.

³ For this is good and acceptable in the sight of God our Savior:(KJV).

God calls you to grow where He plants you, in every season, even if you don't understand why you are there. The key to getting to the next level and dimension is not found in complaining about it or dishonoring the authority that God has placed over you.

Rather, *the **key to promotion is praise**!* Firstly, God has you there for a reason. You are to learn something from the person (or people) put in position over you. Somehow, rather good or bad stimulus, it will produce something of value in you, as God is building your content and even character. This might look like something as simple as, in the case of bad leadership, God training and pruning *your* own character and how you react. Will you allow bad leadership to pull you out of character?? On the flip side, maybe God is testing, will you allow bad leadership to corrupt you? Or will you will able to withstand the corrupt environment and stay true to God? (Think like the Prophet Daniel in the book of Daniel. He served under evil kings, yet his heart, will, and disposition remained in God. He remained obedient to God and did not let the evil kings corrupt him; rather he remained in God and allowed God to use him to perfect God's Will in him and through him). On the other spectrum, you could be placed under excellent leadership for God to model excellence for you and to train you up in excellence. The list goes on.

If you don't learn whatever it is that God intended for you to learn from that particular person or position, God will allow you to continue to encounter those same type of people and those same positions, or same places. So instead of complaining and being bitter, be thankful to God for where you are and thankful for what He is *building* in you. Praise God for promotion! To praise God means to call attention to the glory of God. Humble yourself and **exalt** *God.* Humble your circumstances and exalt God!

"Complain and remain, or praise and be raised!" (Joyce Meyers)

Magnify God, instead of magnifying circumstances or self!

God is bigger than any circumstances that you may face. Take David and Goliath, for instance. He fought lions and bears that seemed big to a small shepherd boy. He defeated the lion and bear (with what he had) and went on to fight Goliath. The lions and bears was preparation for Goliath. Goliath seemed bigger in stature and bigger than anything that David possessed to defeat Goliath with (so it appeared). However, because David did not measure his success based on his tools, and he trusted God for strategy and direction, David gained victory over Goliath. He kept a correct perspective, which was this: although Goliath was big, God was, is, and forever will be BIGGER!

What problem are you facing that seems "too big?" *Put it into perspective.* Don't tell God how big your problems are. TELL your problems how BIG your GOD is! Praise and magnify GOD-not the problem, not even yourself. Don't magnify your feelings, wants or desires over the process or over God. God tells us that we must decrease so that He must increase (John 3:30).

Stop making things about yourself and how you feel or how it affects you. Don't walk in your flesh or feelings. Instead, walk continually in The Spirit. "If we live in The Spirit, let us *walk* in The Spirit." (Galatians 5:25) Watch then, how small your giant becomes.

Adopt a Spirit of Gratitude, instead of being critical or complaining.

There is something supernatural that happens when you can look a giant in the eye and still praise God! Your praise frustrates the enemy. The enemy is counting on you to be sad, depressed, discouraged, distracted,…etc. He wants you to complain. However, when you stay focused on God and not the storm, and when you adopt a *sincere* spirit of gratitude instead of complaining, God honors that. When you continue steadfastly in the Lord and remain faithful with where you are, **God honors your process with promotion.**

1 Corinthians 15:58 tells us, "be ye unshakeable, immoveable, and steadfast in the Lord, for you know that nothing that you do for The Lord is ever in vain." God tells us that if you remain faithful with little, God will make you ruler of much. Matthew 25:23 says, "The master said, 'Well done, my good and faithful servant. You have been faithful in handling this small amount, so now I will give you many more responsibilities. Let's celebrate together!" (NLT)

Before you can become ruler of anything, you have to be a leader and allow God to equip you with the necessary training. You must continue to praise God for the promotion, even when you don't see the promotion coming just yet. All of this is a part of the process which builds value within you for the purpose and position that God has predestined for you long ago.

Duty Fulfilled

We all have great duty to be great in the unique set of greatness that God has ascribed unto us. You, my sister have great virtue within you. You have something special that only you could provide to the world for such a time as this. When you were created, nay before you were created, God had you in mind; He already ordained a specific time for you with a specific calling and a specific plan for a specific purpose. It is in your DNA to be great! Divine Natural Authority given to you is to trample down snakes and scorpions and to cast out demons. God created you to rise above the chaos, distress and defeat, and to rise into victory that is in CHRIST. The world would have you think that this is your life and that you can do whatever you want, whenever you want and there would be no consequences. The world wants you to live life aimlessly from one frivolous thing to the next, all in the name of "fun".

Truth is, your actions do have consequences. Every action that you complete has *eternal significance*, as well as, impacts those around you. We are not as independent as the world wants us to be or says that we are. The system of the world and its way of thinking creates division amongst everyone. It is true that God gives you free will to decide to live life for yourself or to live life for Him, as He intended, but don't play into the world's philosophy or way of thinking, or being. That is the anti-Christ spirit that seeks to lead you astray from Christ. The world says, 'yolo'-you only live once, so do what makes you feel comfortable." Following CHRIST is not always comfortable, but it is necessary and well worth it. Sometimes, you will be comfortable, following Christ, and other times you will experience discomfort (just as with anything else).

If you decide to forsake God and the process that He is leading you through, what would you being doing for your current or future generations, while you seek to please self or the world? What legacy are you leaving behind, not just for yourself, but for God's Kingdom and for the glory of God?

Mark 3:25 Tells us, "And if a house be divided against itself, that house cannot stand". (KJV)

Matthew 12:25 also states" And Jesus knew their thoughts, and said unto them, every kingdom divided against itself is brought to desolation; and every city or house divided against itself shall not stand". (KJV)

This is exactly what the enemy would want to happen. Instead of you playing into that whole "yolo" thing or trying to live your life for yourself, choose to fulfill your duty as Christ calls you to do so. Be the team player that God calls you to be on His team. Don't think only about yourself. When you truly live for God, you no longer belong to self, but to God. Your life becomes poured out for God, just as Christ was poured out for us all. God calls you and created you to be a part of something great beyond yourself. We're talking about *eternal* matters-yes, eternity. Don't spend your life building your own castle at the expense of forsaking God's Kingdom. When you first build God's Kingdom, He includes your castle-it comes with the territory and is much bigger than anything that you could build on your own. "Except the LORD build the house, they labor in vain that build it..." Psalm 127:1 (KJV)

God created you to fit into and be a part of the body of Christ, standing in unity-to stand out against the world and its deception. When you fulfill your piece of the "big picture", it all comes together. When you discover purpose and God's plans for your life, and fully and freely walk in that greatness, God is honored; your soul is fulfilled and your purpose and destiny is manifested. Your soul is most fulfilled when it is doing what it was created to do!

Don't hide behind the shades of fear or uncertainty; BE BOLD. Take a stand and BE BRAVE. Joshua 1:9 says, "This is my command—be strong and courageous! Do not be afraid or discouraged. For the LORD your God is with you wherever you go." (NLT)

Habakkuk 3:19 says, "The LORD God is my strength, and he will make my feet like hinds' feet, and he will make me to walk upon mine high places." (KJV)

Joshua 1:3 says, "Every place that the sole of your foot shall tread upon, that have I given unto you, as I said unto Moses". (KJV)

Yes, this journey, this life, the calling, it all feels daunting at one time or another, but God has especially equipped you with the tools necessary to do His Will and to fulfill your duty. This comes through the process and builds value in you for God's Kingdom. Think of it as "on-the-job-training" for the actual job. All those trials, difficult people, and difficult things build your character and content. God allows you to go through certain situations to prepare you for your destiny. He is preparing you for the position that He has uniquely carved out just for you. People and places are stalled right now, waiting for you! It could possibly be that you are in a particular part of the process that prepares you for a future position or a future time. Either way, it all goes along with God's timeline and God's plan.

You have a duty to God to not abandon the process that prepares you for your purpose, when you choose to follow Christ. When you follow JESUS, you are saying, "Yes, LORD, I will do what you have called me to do." (not out of religious pursuit, but out of a pure heart of love and worship.) John 14:23 Says, Jesus replied, "All who love me will do what I say. My Father will love them, and we will come and make our home with each of them." (NLT)

When you follow JESUS, you are also saying, "I will endure and successfully go through the process that is required for both the purpose and the promotion. Not only will I go through, but I will *grow* through."

Luke 9:23 says, "if any man comes after me, let him deny himself, pick up his cross and follow me". There will be times, when a mountain seems to block the very road that you have to travel, appearing to cut off all access. You have a duty to God, yourself, and everyone who will be impacted by who and what God has called out of you. Don't rob the world, yourself, nor God of being the greatest version of yourself that God saw when He created you before the beginning of time. Do not settle for mediocrity. Transverse to higher levels into the greatness of God that will be manifested in and through you. God requires you to continually travel to a higher level. Let God take you to the places that only He can take you-the places where you cannot get to yourself, without God. Even if you managed to get there without God, you could not withstand the pressure. Your gifting can only take you to a place, but it is your character that will keep you there.

Let's RECAP.

1. The process prepares you for purpose.
2. The promotion leads to position. The position is the avenue by which purpose is fulfilled. God gives you position to fulfill the *mission.*
3. Without the process and without God, you may get the promotion, but the pressure will crush you.
4. Without process, your gifting will bring you to a position where your character cannot sustain or keep you.

Remember, the process builds your character. You have a duty to the process. You have a duty to not abandon the process for comfort, when you experience discomfort at times. At times, the process gets difficult and uncomfortable and we want to quit or slack in the process-we want the easiest way out with the least amount of pain and the least amount of hassle. The world encourages this and entices you to leave the process for comfort. The world promotes instant gratification and speaks against delayed gratification which is essential during the process. What lives in comfort? Death! Death lives in comfort when you choose comfort over the process-where you get too comfortable with where you are and something dies within you.

The very thing that needed the pressure of the process in order to birth your greatness is suppressed when you choose comfort over the process. Think like pressure of coal to become a diamond. Without the pressure on the coal, the coal may be comfortable without that pressure, but never turns into a diamond. The greatness within you dies, or lays dormant rather, when you stop working through the process-when you just sit in the discouragement, in the depression, in the...etc. That is what the enemy wants. He tries to wear you down during the process. He wants you to quit because if you quit the process and take the easy way out, you will miss out on the equipping, on the growth, on the character building, etc.

Now, don't get me wrong, living a life for Christ is not all about pain and the process. It is not all about discomfort. I am simply painting a picture of what it means and what it looks like when you stick to the process for those times that are uncomfortable and painful. As a Christian, there will be times of comfort and times of discomfort-times of happiness and times of sadness...etc.

This is my point, this book has several themes from different perspectives, all centered around you choosing to invest in your own value and purpose through the process, instead of waiting for someone to validate your value or worthiness of being chosen, to live out your purpose and greatness in your life.

The point is that you are already chosen. GOD chose you. You just have to follow His example and choose to perceive and believe in that same worth and value that God has placed within you. A huge part of you choosing yourself is you choosing to fulfill the duty of your God-given calling, purpose, and destiny. You have to choose the process-grow in maturity and embrace the process, instead of abandoning it. It is true that the process builds and stores the essential within you.

These same "essentials" are the very things that God uses to *propel* you into Destiny-into that position to fulfill the mission and purposes of God. In the process of you fulfilling the mission and purpose that God has placed in your life, God is also working things out for *your* good. "All things work together for the good of those who love God and who are called according to His purpose." (Romans 8:28) It's just like any job in the world- only better and it's the best investment you could make when the job is working for God and following Christ. Just like in the natural world, you work your way up to position and that position has perks, God does the same thing, but much better!

You scratch His back! He will scratch yours! "Seek ye first, the Kingdom of God and His righteousness, and all else will be unto you". (Matthew 6:33) When you follow Christ and build God's Kingdom first and foremost, over your own castle, God will then expand your territory and cause all else to fall right into place in your own life. God takes great care of His people. It becomes a mutual benefit.

Just as you invest in yourself so that you can add more value to any company in the natural world, in spiritual terms, if you invest in yourself and choose to go (and grow) through the process, you get value added to you. You can then add this value to God's Kingdom.

At the end of the day, don't you want to hear those amazing words from God, "well done, my good and faithful servant; you can come on in and great is your reward!"

Paul said it best when he wrote, "I have fought the good fight, I have finished the race, and I have remained faithful." (2 Timothy 4:7) (NLT)

Fulfill your duty, my sister, and let God have all the glory! Amen!

Chapter 5:

Commit to Choosing "You" by Choosing CHRIST First!"

Your Value is <u>Not</u> a License to Selfishness

Throughout this book, I have been telling you that you should choose "you"-yourself. We talked also about the process that is *vital* to building those necessary traits and the value that you need to possess in both choosing yourself, and adding value to God and others. The purpose of this section of the chapter is to qualify the basis of the concept of "choosing yourself". **While choosing yourself is important, it is equally as important to mention that choosing yourself DOES NOT mean being selfish or idolizing yourself over God and His plans.** Choosing yourself first, does not mean that you put yourself ahead of everything and everyone, as you try to get ahead with a spirit of selfishness and pride.

Choosing yourself simply means that you take the initiative to choose to invest in yourself and pursue God's purpose for life. It's about investing in yourself to pursue all of the amazingly wonderful dreams that God has placed in your heart. It's about investing in the person that is you. If I gave you a brand new Mercedes and then gave you a used thunderbird car, which one would you invest time into cleaning? You would take the upmost responsibility and give the best care to the Mercedes to make sure that it maintained its value right? Well, you are that Mercedes. That means that just as you would most likely care for that car, you and your body are the Temple that you need to care for. Invest in your appearance. Invest in your emotions. Invest in your mental capacity. Invest in your Spirituality-your relationship with God through Jesus. Invest in the process of pursuing and preparing for purpose and greatness!

This book is about you investing in all of the beforementioned, in investing in yourself, rather than waiting for someone to deem you worthy enough to be invested in. Instead of waiting for someone to recognize your value, YOU recognize your value! Choose yourself when no one else chooses you! I want to encourage you to still be kind; stay rooted and grounded in God's love, as you transverse through the process of building self-value and choosing yourself in all areas of your life.

On your way to the top, don't be that person who says, "the ends justify the means". That pretty much says that anything goes, no matter the cost. That mentality and attitude says that it does not matter who gets hurt in the process, as long as you get what you need or want. This is NOT of God and is not the way of CHRIST! That mentality and attitude is not cool and is not the true meaning of choosing yourself.

God calls you to a standard of grace and love-to be fair in all of your doings and being. God calls you to have a *higher standard* than that of the world! Do not take on their selfish mentality or ways.

I encourage you to get with GOD and determine what your core values are. (this is a 3rd type of value that I did not go much into with this particular book) What are your principles? Ask yourself what are you willing to do and not willing to do to get to the top? Where do you draw the line? Do you and will you still operate with Godly moral, character, and integrity? Or will you compromise your Christian beliefs, character, and value, and do whatever is "necessary", no matter how wrong it is, just to advance yourself?

The point is that there is a right way and a wrong way in choosing yourself. The wrong way is to mistreat people or to use people in order to get to where you want to be.

As you build value, remember, it is not all about you. God wants to use you. He wants to utilize the value that HE has invested in you throughout the process, in order to add value to others and His Kingdom. The added value is for you AND others. God tells us in 2 Corinthians 1:4, "He comforts us in all our troubles so that we can comfort others. When they are troubled, we will be able to give them the same comfort God has given us." (NLT)

That same process that added value to you is what makes up part of your anointing. You can then add value to, and minister to others from the place of your experience and process. Remember, the whole goal of life as a Christian is to expand and further GOD'S Kingdom, all for HIS glory. We can still have well-balanced, fulfilling and fun lives outside of business and ministry, but at the end of the day, life really isn't about us, our emotions, our feelings or desires; it's about God.

(by the way, ministry is not just mission trips and nonprofit organizations. As a Christian, ministry is your everyday interactions and wherever God leads you)

God says in His word that we must decrease so that He may increase. Think of how your life will be as a living sacrifice and obedient purpose for God's

Kingdom. You are the Vessel for GOD'S Will, and *love* manifested to others. God just loves you enough to allow you to be fulfilled as well.

His word and purpose are always a two-edged sword-a two way street. All things work together for the good of those who love God and who are called according to His purpose. He takes all of your struggles, trials, triumphs,... etc, to build something beautiful in you, so that He can work <u>through</u> you, and even <u>for</u> you.

So, as you choose yourself, remember to first choose God and His purpose for your life. Choose and seek GOD's Will. Matthew 6:33 says, "seek ye first the Kingdom of God and His righteousness, and all these things shall be added unto you." (KJV). If you go after the other things first before God, you become an idolater of those things (and people), at the risk of forsaking God. You will surely lose all those things/people in that case. However, when you seek after God first, with a sincere heart of worship for the heart of God, and not the hand of God, you not only get God and purpose, but God includes all those other things as a package. (This topic could go much deeper, but I will stop at this point).

Don't wait for others to invest in God's purpose or Will for you. If you know that God is calling you to do something, find a way! Adopt a mindset and spirit of resourcefulness. Invest in the vision that God has given you!

Continue to love yourself and others in the process, as you love and pursue God. Continue to serve others and to add value to them. Don't forget to treat yourself nicely as well and to add value unto yourself- You cannot pour out of an empty vessel; you need balance and time to refresh in the presence of The Lord.

As you add more value to yourself, you become more valuable (same inherent value, more added value) and then have more value to add. Soon after, others will start to add value to you because of what you sow. You may or may not reap it from the same field that you sow, but you will reap it from somewhere! So, you want more real love, then serve and love others with a real, authentic love. Then others will serve and love you with real, authentic love. You attract what is inside of you-good or bad.

Before others can perceive your real value, you have to first perceive your own value. You need to properly carry and properly present it. You need to know it, practice it and own it. You need to manifest and fully and confidently walk in it! Then others will start to see and appreciate that value. I have surely learned this for myself and have lived on all ends of the spectrum. I tell you all of this from a place of experience, growth, and maturity. Once you own your own value, then others will start to see and appreciate that value, though there will be some that just will refuse to recognize true value, because they don't see it in themselves (a different story altogether).

So, don't be selfish with the value that you are building within and what God is building within you. Share that value where it is needed and where God leads you to sow that value. Do not stop the flow of what God is doing in you. Don't hinder the flow of the anointing. The value that you are building and that you possess is not just for you. It is meant to flow <u>through</u> you to reach others, not to just stop with you. Seek God for wisdom and guidance through the process. Ask Him where the value is needed. Also, pray for balance and for discernment; you do not want to sow your hard earned value just to anyone or anywhere. God also says, in Matthew 7:6, "Don't waste what is holy on people who are unholy. Don't throw your pearls to pigs! They will trample the pearls, then turn and attack you." (NLT)

Know your value. Practice your value. OWN your value. Share your value with wisdom.

Steward Your Value

No matter where you are in your journey with perceiving and building value for purpose, continue to fine tune yourself with self-development. Know your strengths and weaknesses and allow God to continue to mold, shape, and prepare you for where He is taking you! Greatness demands and requires it!

Continue to hone your craft. Be disciplined-walk in the discipline that it takes to be great. Just as you would work towards a better version of yourself and endure the process for someone else to choose you (whether that be a spouse, a job,...etc) you must continue in your process of self-improvement/self-development, with God as the Master Potter. It is *your* responsibility to steward the gifts and talents that God has so graciously blessed you with. As you build value through the process of character building, do not give that value away inappropriately (not in relationships, careers,...etc).

Stand firm in your value, keenly perceive your value through the eyes of God and with the mind of Christ. Trust in the value that you and God have partnered in investing in. Practice that value. Freely and **confidently** *walk* in the value that you bring! Let your actions, thoughts, and character echo that value! Own your value! Do not rent your value to anyone, whether that be in relationships, in business, career,…etc. Stand firm and *absolute* in holding the keys to your value and your future!

Don't allow other people, or even circumstance, to dictate your value. You've worked through the process of self-improvement/development and equipping and you are inherently valuable. Continue to faithfully practice those things that are necessary toward success! Remember, success is a series of small action steps that add into a compound of larger success. You won't get there overnight, but step by step, faith by faith, God will carry you and you will get there!

Examine each area of your life. What do you want to see happen in your family relationships? Your other relationships? Your friendships, your business relationships? Your self-relationship? Your relationship with God/Jesus/Holy Spirit?

Now think about the value that you bring and provide to each of those. Remember, even when none of those relationships choose you (excluding your relationship with God-He chose you first!)...

YOU still choose "you"-yourself!

Choose to appreciate and honor the value that you own. Steward the treasure of your value that resulted from the process of daily activities-the value that resulted from the trials, difficulties, and refinement. Even though you feel alone at times throughout the process of difficulty, always remember that we all have our own process. Continue to be humble and remember that your process, nor your destiny is no more important or superior to anyone else; on the flip side, no other person's process and destiny is more important than yours. We all have a part in the Kingdom and we are all loved by God. This is a great mentality and spirit to steward, along with the stewardship of undergoing your process.

Allow God to continue to mold and shape you into what He had in mind from the beginning of time. As you learn to see yourself through the eyes and heart of GOD, you will begin to operate in all of the before-mentioned relationships differently. You will operate from the core and capacity of the true value that you have to add. You will no longer rely on those relationships (except for with God) to validate you or your worth, competence, ability, etc.

Invest in yourself. Allow God to invest in you and make your dreams and destiny a *reality*! Manifest your greatness within! Your value and content which is developed through the process is what builds that greatness in you. It propels you into destiny and even more greatness. Don't wait around to receive permission from others for you to choose yourself and to manifest greatness. Instead, manifest that greatness by first perceiving and believing in your own value. Choose yourself when others don't notice or choose you. Choose the process over comfort. Don't be defined by other's limited perception of you. Choose GOD's view of you! Operate in *that* capacity! Bravely chart the course that God has pre-mapped out for you. Don't wait for life to happen. YOU make life happen! You choose "you"!

THE END……..

THE BEGINNING OF YOUR NEW LIFE!!!!!!!!!!!!!!!!

Epilogue:

Dear Sister,

      I am sure that after you have read this book, you have gone through a series of different emotions-some good, some bad. My prayer for you is that you have found real value in this book and a real love encounter with the Lover of your soul, who is JESUS. I pray that the knowledge and insight that you have gained, plants firm roots of love and value in your heart and life. Wherever you may find yourself in knowing your value, please know, and always remember that you are worthy to be chosen-even if you are the person, choosing you! GOD has already chosen you and has *marked* you as His-His Royal Priesthood. So, follow God's footsteps. You do the same-you choose "you"-yourself!

CHAPTER 3 WORKSHEET (ACCESS THE PROCESS):

Worth Application Category Assessment:

There are **4 main categories** that you may fall into when it comes to how you perceive and apply your worth:

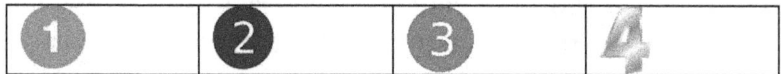

1	2	3	4

Category 1. You don't know your worth at all.

Category 2: You know your worth, but don't Practice or Own it.

Category 3: You Know and Practice your worth, but do not fully own it. You sometimes transfer ownership of your value to others. ("you <u>rent </u>the Mercedes")

Category 4: You Know, Practice and successfully OWN your own value. ("you <u>own</u> the Mercedes")

Answer the questions below very honestly to get your accurate self-assessment of <u>which category</u> you fall into, in regards to how you perceive and apply your worth. (There will be a short series of questions broken down into 3 broad areas:

- Life (section 1)

- Work (section2)

-Relationships (section 3)

Each section has 4 statements (A through D). For each of the 4 statements (A through D) under each section, <u>circle</u> the statement that you **Most agree** with. Once you complete the three sections (Life, Work, Relationships), get your results on the next page entitled, "**Solution Sheet. Interpreting Your Results:**"

Section 1-LIFE:

(circle **1 out of the 4** statements that is MOST true.)

Statement A: I believe that I should accept whatever life throws at me, because in this life, you get what comes to you.

Statement B: I believe that I deserve more in life, but I am **not** actively in pursuit of better things in life.

Statement C: I both know that I deserve more in life AND I definitely work at getting better in life. I know that I am worth more in life, but I just have to wait for the right opportunities and people to recognize me, in order to advance and get better quality.

Statement D: I Confidently know that I deserve the absolute best in life and wait for no one or nothing to recognize what I am worth. I actively pursue my own goals and passion in life and create my own opportunities to get the life of quality that I desire and deserve.

Section 2-WORK:

(circle **1 out of the 4** statements that is MOST true.)

Statement A: I am selective in the type of job that I accept, but **not** selective in my pay as much as I can be.

Statement B: I do not accept just any job. I usually negotiate my pay, but only if my employer invites me to negotiate.

Statement C: I typically accept whatever work I can find. After all, today's economy is bad and I am just lucky to be working.

Statement D: I am very conscientious of the types of jobs that I even apply for. The job has to match my qualifications, skills, and pay requirement If I am going to invest any time or effort.

Section 3-RELATIONSHIPS:

(circle **1 out of the 4** statements that is MOST true.)

Statement A: I <u>always</u>, <u>every time</u>, attract low quality relationships, especially those of the opposite sex. Guys address me in a disrespectful way. I usually accept the first guy that comes along because I never know when the next one will come and I have to take what I can get.

Statement B: I attract high quality relationships (personal and business, family and "romantic"). Everyone in my relationships treat me with the upmost respect and honor. They invite and value my opinions, and sometimes implements my ideas.

Statement C: I MORE OFTEN than not, attract low to medium quality relationships. I try anything to catch a guy's attention, just as long as he notices me.

Statement D: I attract decent quality relationships. When it especially comes to a man, I let him pursue me, but I have the tendency to experience emotional rollercoaster based on our interactions, or the lack thereof.

Solution Sheet. Interpreting Your Results:

(You should have **only 1** out of every 4 statements circled for each section)

Section 1-LIFE:

If you circled:

- Statement A, you are in **Category 1**
- Statement B, you are in **Category 2**
- Statement C, you are in **Category 3**
- Statement D, you are in **Category 4**

Please refer to the title worksheet, "worth application category assessment" to be reminded of what each category is.

Write out your Worth Application Category number for (LIFE) here:

_____

Section2-WORK:

If you circled:

- Statement A, you are in **Category 2**
- Statement B, you are in **Category 3**
- Statement C, you are in **Category 1**
- Statement D, you are in **Category 4**

Write out your worth application Category number for (WORK) here:

_____

Section 3-RELATIONSHIPS:

If you circled:

- Statement A, you are in **Category 1**
- Statement B, you are in **Category 4**
- Statement C, you are in **Category 2**
- Statement D, you are in **Category 3**

Write out your Worth Application Category number for (RELATIONSHIPS) here:

_____

Quick Recap: Now write out your 3 scores for each of the 3 sections to see them all in one place:

LIFE: _____

WORK: _____

RELATIONSHIPS: _____

> *****Note: You may have the same score in all 3 areas or you may have different scores in different areas. ******

www.ingramcontent.com/pod-product-compliance
Lightning Source LLC
Chambersburg PA
CBHW071058090426
42737CB00013B/2376